ZERO2HIRED

Successfully Break Through Your Interview Process

By

John Ribeiro & Connel Valentine

ZERO2HIRED

Successfully Break Through Your Interview Process

www.zero2hired.com

Editor: Zoë C. Waller

Library and Archives Canada Cataloguing in Publication

Ribeiro, John (John Charles), author
   Zero2Hired : successfully break through your interview process / by John Ribeiro & Connel Valentine.

Issued in print and electronic formats.
ISBN 978-0-9959627-0-5 (softcover).--ISBN 978-0-9959627-1-2 (ebook)

   1. Job hunting--Handbooks, manuals, etc. 2. Career development--Handbooks, manuals, etc. I. Valentine, Connel, author II. Title. III. Title: Zero 2 hired. IV. Title: Zero to hired.

HF5382.7.R5 2017   650.14084'2   C2017-903808-7
                                           C2017-903809-5

Dedicated to hardworking Millennials

who are discovering their purpose and striving to reach their potential.

TABLE OF CONTENTS

INTRODUCTION

It's 10:00 on a Monday morning. Time to hop onto your favourite job search websites and see what's biting today. You've been at it for weeks, even months, and you've not received a single call back. Or maybe you've had a couple of phone conversations with recruiters who left you with "We'll get back to you," but you've heard nothing. You've crossed your fingers for so long, they're now stuck in a knot. But you tell yourself that *today* is the day. You'll apply for five or six different jobs online, and somebody will call you, right?

What if we told you that what you're doing is the probably the most *damaging, unproductive* waste of time for your career? What if we told you that the job postings you see online do not represent a large percentage of what's really available in the large and mostly hidden job market? What if we told you that you may be applying to positions that have already been filled? What if we told you that hiring managers and recruiters may not even be looking at your application? Would you lose sleep over it? We hope so, because it's time to wake up and realize that you're putting your energy and your faith in a hiring process that is broken.

Millennials, the up-and-comers of our workforce, are experiencing the hardships of uncertainty at this time. With two major economic crises within a decade (set off by the Dot Com Bubble burst in 2000 and the real estate-based financial crisis in 2008), in traditional terms, the concept of *job security* is now a myth. Millennials today face massive student loans to repay, are moving back in with their parents, and are taking on survival jobs just to make ends meet. In the January 2017 release of the labour force survey by Statistics Canada (**statcan.gc.ca**), unemployment among young people aged 15 to 24 increased by 0.7 per cent to 13.3 per cent in Canada, with little change on both a monthly and year-over-year basis.

You Millennials have courage. That is, the courage to pay your way through postsecondary education and postgraduate education that have typically increased by a whopping 16.8 and 18.3 per cent respectively over the past five years alone. Many of you have also shown the courage to move to a new country in the pursuit of an education or a better life. Millennials possess untapped potential to contribute to our workforce in better ways than previous generations did. All too often, however, the hiring process itself stands in your way.

Technology has crippled the now self-contradictory hiring process. Ask hiring managers what they look for in the people they hire, and you will hear, "I seek the right personality" (or a variation of this theme). Yet, the recruitment method of choice is an online system (a.k.a. Application Tracking System or ATS) to filter applicants through to the interview stage. Can you honestly rely on a computer to score your personality? No, you can't. What an ATS system does accomplish very well, however, is generating volume, making the process a heck of a lot easier for recruiters with targets based on hiring volume. Scores of job-hungry candidates catapult their resumés onto the cyber wall with the hope that at least one will stick. This process does nothing to connect the right people with the right jobs, yet this has become the default method for most companies. What's even more unsettling, it's a process with which most Millennials are completely comfortable.

Zero2Hired is written to explain how you can work around this broken process to get the job you deserve, as well as to reveal what's on the other side of that Submit button. This book has been written by two hiring managers with over 30 years of combined experience who know exactly what's going on behind the scenes. It will guide you through creating your own back entrance to your next job. If you've applied to tens or maybe hundreds of online job postings with no results, you begin to realize that *you* are probably doing something wrong.

So, unless you want to spend the next few months following the same broken process you faithfully used the last hundred times, it's time to change your game. We are here to show you how the *real* game is played. Interestingly enough, Statistics Canada reveals that unemployment rates are steadily *decreasing* for those between the ages of 25 and 54, while fact, a 2016 survey conducted by **Toronto.ca** showed an *increase* in jobs by 2.7 per cent. *Those who know how the game is played* are filling these positions, and it's time that you found a piece of the action.

Zero2Hired will guide you from the moment you start seriously considering your options and preparing your resumé to the moment you begin settling into your new job. Creating your resumé is just the start; passing it into the right hands is key. Next, acing the interview will land you the job. Finally, working your way competently through the probation period will help you to keep that job.

Your two authors, John Ribeiro and Connel Valentine have different backgrounds and expertise that are consolidated here for your benefit.

A new immigrant to Canada, Connel Valentine researched the subject of job searching for a year before he moved here. With no North American work experience, he put his research into practice and nabbed a job at a level that acknowledged the breadth of his international experience, at one of the largest enterprises in Canada. The process took just over two weeks—a story that most immigrants would find hard to believe!

John Ribeiro is a hiring process veteran who has interviewed hundreds of job applicants. There once came a time in his IT industry career when upper management decided that the jobs of 25 IT analysts on his team were to be outsourced six months later. John responded by slapping on his leadership hat and coaching his team on the techniques for acing interviews. Within six months, every one of those 25 employees had a new job, and they weren't fired—they fired their company instead!

To make things easier for you, this book presents the steps for your enhanced job application process in chronological order. This is a common sense, process-based approach to landing your next job as quickly as possible. You will find no secret formulas and no find-your-passion, follow-your-dream messages in here. There are no lists to write or journal entries to create. You will only create lists that contribute to your resumé or your interview skills. Time is of the essence. Every day that you're not working, you're missing out on opportunities. While bankers are smiling at the interest piling up on your loan, the business world is devoid of your talents. Our goal is to get you into the workforce ASAP!

There is one caveat—a prerequisite and acknowledgement you must accept before you read the first chapter. We are not here to make your life easier. In fact, we will be making it *harder*. Job searching is a job. JOB SEARCHING IS A JOB! This means that you must dedicate substantial time in your day toward your job search process. We know that it can be frustrating to spend so much time on unpaid activity, especially when a world of entertainment from social media and on-demand TV is only a screen tap away, but you must make a choice now before continuing on. Either you dedicate more hours *per day* to your job search, or you will be spending more *weeks* or *months* unemployed or underemployed.

The authors of this book have made a promise to help Millennials get the job they deserve. Now it's your turn to make a promise to yourself that you will now place a clear and dedicated focus on your career. You will prove to yourself that those stereotypical labels of "lazy", "entitled", and "seeking instant gratification" aren't true and don't matter. So, if you're ready to put down your Smartphone, roll up your sleeves, and get to work… let's begin!

CHAPTER 1

DEBUNKING THE MYTHS

Before we start, we need to clear the air on certain preconceived notions you may have. A dangerous gap between reality and fiction exists. It is based on misconceptions and assumptions that we should address before proceeding.

Many of the points below may either come as a pleasant surprise to you or be downright shocking. Remember that these revelations are based on facts and our collective experience in the *real* corporate world. From all the many Millennials (also known as Gen Y) we have already coached, we hear repeating patterns of doubt and uncertainty that only serve to hold these job seekers back.

In this first chapter, we ask that you first examine then jettison the myths to which you have been clinging. You need to clear your mind and prepare yourself for the fresh start in your new career journey that will begin in the chapters to follow.

Myth: You need to have experience

So, you're looking through public job postings and reading through swarms of job descriptions. At some point, you're thinking *I don't have enough experience* or *I don't have the skills they're looking for.*

The job description you're reading was created by someone—most likely the hiring manager or supervisor with help from the human resources recruiter. It could comprise three sections:

> 1. Job Functions: the responsibilities of the job that will make up your day-to-day activities
> 2. Education: the formal college or university education or specialized courses
> 3. Soft Skills: skills that are innate to your personality that enable you to work well with other people (e.g., communication or organization skills)

When this job description is drawn up, it reflects a wish list of both must-haves and nice-to-haves. For entry-level to mid-management roles, the employer does not, in reality, expect to find someone to fulfil 100 per cent of these so-called requirements. At most, the hiring manager expects compliance of around 70 per cent.

Unfortunately, job descriptions don't formally distinguish the must-haves from the nice-to-haves on their websites. (Wouldn't that be convenient?) Luckily, it's easy to identify the must-haves—these are the requirements that appear at the top of the list.

Following the 70-per-cent rule, when there are 10 job functions listed in the job description, the hiring manager should consider anyone who can do the first five to seven. If there are four requirements for education, with say, a bachelor's degree in computer science being the first, that's probably all they need.

Do employers do this intentionally? No, they don't. It's human nature to present the most relevant requirements for any need at the top of the list. What do you notice about your grocery list? Items you need the most—milk, eggs, bread, produce—tend to find themselves at the top of the list. The items you could do without or use less often tend to appear at the bottom.

The most qualified candidate does not necessarily get the job. Employers are first and foremost looking for a person who is a *cultural* fit with the company and the team. That is, the candidate with the right *attitude* and *personality* to suit the job. From personal experience, both of us can tell you that our biggest hiring regrets were not from employees who could not *functionally* do the job, but from employees who had bad attitudes, did not get along well with others, or just did not seem engaged with their work.

We once hired a Millennial on our team whose IT experience had been limited to working on IT projects in college. His prior job had been as a baggage handler at the airport. Although we had some concern about his lack of professional IT experience, this candidate had an outgoing personality, a willingness to learn, and a can-do attitude—so we gave him a chance. He turned out to be one of our best analysts.

Now by no means are we completely eliminating the value of experience from your profile. Hiring managers will be partial to candidates brimming with experience in the responsibilities stated in the job description. (We will cover the possibilities of obtaining experience later on, but for now, understand that the necessity for experience can be overstated.) Don't be intimidated by the years of experience and must-haves listed in the job description. You can still win a hiring manager's trust, even if you lack experience.

Myth: You don't have the right qualifications

In many industries, especially IT, there is no shortage of specialized courses out there. There are courses in everything from Cisco and Microsoft through to project management and Six Sigma. The list is endless. Recruiters and job seekers alike love to splash their job descriptions and resumés with these ambitious titles.

Now, by no means are we belittling these qualifications. They do add value and demonstrate a willingness to learn, which are important factors. But in reality, the *application* of what is taught in these courses is extremely rare. There are, however, exceptions in certain industries.

While it is commendable to those who have learned something through these courses, the fact remains that most people in the field have acquired the majority of their technical knowledge from their own hands-on experience. Highly specialized fields such as medicine, law and others are exceptions. Even large enterprises do not follow the standards and best practices taught in these courses. They may use these standards and practices as guidelines, but many managers often go with their gut.

Because of this, hiring managers do not attach as much importance to these qualifications on a resumé as you would think. When we look at a resumé, we skim over the certifications that the candidate proudly displays, unless it's a qualification that is really essential to the job, such as a PMP certification for a Project Management position.

So why are you seeing it on the job description? Are these qualifications just smoke and mirrors? As we said before, job descriptions are wish lists. It's nice to have someone who is ITIL (Information Technology Infrastructure Library) certified on our team. But between the overly confident ITIL-certified candidate, and the passionate non-certified candidate, we'll choose the latter.

Now that you know this, you also know that there is no need to feel *intimidated* by the qualification requirements you see on a job description. That being said, *don't neglect obtaining certification.* If you see the same qualification over and over on job descriptions for the same type of role, take the hint—it's probably a minimal requirement.

Myth: There are not enough jobs

Hiring never stops. Hiring **never** stops! No matter what is going on in the world economically, there are **always** jobs available. So, to keep telling yourself and others, *I'm not getting a job because times are tough,* is a lame excuse for not putting in the effort required to follow the methodologies outlined in this book. Don't blame it on luck either. *Successful people make their own luck.*

Of course, during economic downturns, job cuts will occur. According to statistics from **Toronto.ca**, between October 2008 and 2009, there were 400,000 job cuts, amounting to a 2.3 per cent loss in the city. Certain industries were more affected than others; the manufacturing sector accounted for more than half of this percentage.

But the need to hire is always there. Companies are always expanding and creating new positions:

> 1. Employees are leaving or being promoted, creating a vacuum down the line to be filled
> 2. New initiatives are being taken, creating new positions in existing departments
> 3. New start-ups by bold entrepreneurs need like-minded individuals to join their team and take on a new challenge.

The job market holds discouraging truths as well.

Many job opportunities are **not** advertised. Yes, you read that right! For example, when a new position is available, larger companies may make it mandatory to hire internally only, or at least advertise the position internally for a few weeks before making the position available publicly. It's always cheaper and less risky for the employer to hire from within.

Additionally, some job postings are actually *phantom* positions, for which the employer already has a candidate in mind, but is required by company policy to run through the posting and interview process purely as a formality.

Don't be too discouraged by this. Keep in mind that every person hired internally creates a vacuum somewhere down the line that could be filled by you. As for those phantom positions that you interviewed for, at least you gain interview experience, and if the interviewers liked you, they may keep your file for future reference. That's how Connel's wife got her job.

The best thing you can do for yourself is to ditch the scarcity mentality and start owning an abundance mentality. Plenty of jobs are out there for you, as long as you know how to stand out of the crowd and market your brand. And that's what this book is all about.

Myth: The one-size-fits-all resumé

Here's a reminder of something you already know—people love receiving something personal. It could be a mug with their photo on it, or a 'geotagged' picture (with details such as latitude and longitude, bearing, altitude, distance or place names) on Instagram.

Your resumé and cover letter are no different. Employers want to see a resumé that speaks directly to the company and to the job description of that particular available position. No two employers are looking for the same requirements, even if the job title is the same. While you are considering this, remember that as you change the order and emphasis of your skills, you *must* always remain honest in your resumé.

As a quick example, say you're applying to be a project administrator, and two different companies advertise a position with that job title. One job description lists a requirement for communication skills, while the other lists a requirement for documentation skills. You will customize your resumé by either *excluding* the skill that is not required, or by *reordering* your skills to put the one that is relevant first

Important note: You need to modify your resumé and cover letter for *every* job that you apply to. It's common knowledge that a typical recruiter will take six to 10 seconds to scan your resumé before deciding whether to read on or toss it into the trash. Common sense would thus indicate that you must keep information that is most relevant to the job at the top of each section of your document. (Remember the grocery list?)

Certainly, customization of your resumé and cover letter requires a significant amount of time and commitment during your job search process, but this is where you acquire the payoff. Don't worry, you won't be building a resumé from scratch for every job application. We've got you covered on making this process a whole lot easier. More on this later!

Myth: Applying to 20 postings a day is productive

The previous section may have started you thinking, *If I have to customize my resumé and cover letter for **every** job application, I won't have time to apply for every job I come across. Won't that make me less productive?* Yes and no. You won't be able to apply for 20 jobs per day, but you will definitely be more productive by applying for every job with a targeted and strategic approach. Temptation alert: You may feel that applying for many jobs per day by uploading a generic resumé and clicking Submit is productive, but we guarantee you that the generic-resumé-Submit method will end up *increasing* the time you spend looking for a job.

By applying to two to three *publicly advertised* jobs per day, Connel was able to find work in one of the most prestigious companies in Canada in just over two weeks. This is with no prior work experience in North America. Total number of job applications: fourteen. Total number of offers: three!

By applying for 20 jobs a day, you are essentially choosing quantity over quality (never a good thing). If you're going to bed with a sense of accomplishment, know that your generic resumé is suffocating under a pile of hundreds, maybe even thousands of other resumés for the same job. What's so special about yours that the employer will bother to open it? Are you sure you've nailed the right keywords in the right places for it to rank high enough? And what are the chances that your competition has done the same?

Applying for fewer jobs with a strategic and targeted approach using the methods described in this book will yield more calls for interviews and reduce the painful time spent looking for work. There is much more to a job application than just clicking Submit. All this will be explained later.

Myth: Hand-delivering your resumé at the door works

As we walk by the security desk or the receptionists at our front door, we cringe every time we see a desperate, well-dressed (and misguided) job hunter, dropping off a resumé with the *hopes* it will end up in the hands of a hiring manager. We think of the precious time that these individuals have wasted with this newspaper delivery methodology, time that could have been better spent networking with the very people who have the authority to hire them.

Are you one of these folks? The receptionists or security personnel to whom you've just entrusted your resumé has most likely *not* been given instructions from hiring managers or human resources that they need to entertain these drop offs. In all likelihood, they will accept your documents and tell you what you need to hear so you'll leave. Then they can toss your resumé into the trash and return to their own jobs.

Heading out your door and visiting office after office to deliver your resumé takes time. These are precious hours in your day that could have been spent doing something more productive, such as learning a new skill, finding information about someone to network with, or researching news updates on a company you're interested in working for.

Ditch this desperate door-to-door strategy. It will not work unless you are extremely lucky, or you're looking to work in a retail store.

> Interestingly enough, John got his first job hand-delivering his resumé at an independent computer retail store. However, retail store jobs and office jobs are entirely different ball games. When you walk into a retail store, there's a chance that the person who has the authority to hire you is standing right behind the counter. You then engage in conversation with that person, which was your objective all along.

Myth: Cover letters are not important

As if creating a customized resumé wasn't hard enough, I've got to create a customized cover letter too? Sorry to disappoint some of you, but your cover letter goes hand in hand with your resumé. And no resumé should be submitted without it.

The cover letter is important because it provides you with two opportunities.

Remember what we said about how people are attracted to the *personalized touch*? The cover letter is how you grab the hiring manager's attention, with an attractive and succinct professional comment about the company itself and/or the hiring manager. You don't have this opportunity with your resumé.

The cover letter presents a chance to tell the hiring manager the specific problem you plan to solve. In a nutshell, hiring managers hire people to solve problems. The cover letter allows you to explain how you're going to do that.

The cover letter shouldn't be about you. Rather than focusing on your qualifications and the skills you possess, it's quite the opposite. *It should be about the other person reading it.* Think about it—wouldn't that make a much more engaging and compelling letter to read when it's about the reader and not about you?

Myth: The REAL definition of job security

Although perhaps disappointing, the facts in this section should also come as no surprise. At the very least, here's a wake-up call. The truth is, companies don't *want* you. But, they do *need* you. They need you to solve a problem. Companies have one goal, and one goal *only*—to make money, plain and simple. They make money by selling a product or service, and they make more money by mass selling. Selling products or services is complex. It creates problems and challenges that need to be resolved by a problem-solving engine of employees.

But employees cost money, which eats away at the profit the business is trying to make for its owners and shareholders. If Steve Jobs and "Woz" (Steve Wozniak) could have distributed Apple products to the world without hiring a single employee, they most likely would have. Fortunately for us, business owners need to invest in people to address the complexity faced in distributing their products or services—so they can make more money. Owners also need to keep these people happy, because having to rehire costs money too. But the moment owners find a way to manage and administer their business challenges in a cheaper way, either through automation or outsourcing, "your services are no longer required."

John once lost his team to outsourcing. He had to let go of 25 loyal and hardworking employees, and several other team members from other departments as well. It was the hardest and most challenging time of his career. Some of these people had just bought houses, were raising children and had loans or mortgages to pay off. He's proud that his leadership skills helped all the members on his team to find new jobs before the layoff deadline. Several employees from other teams were not so fortunate.

Is job security a myth? The traditional concept of job security is quickly becoming a thing of folklore. After 15 years of loyalty to their employer, most people like to consider themselves so valued in the organization that they would *never* lose their job. They believe that they have security. But if the company or department they're working for starts to lose money, the security that they take for granted will weaken. Economic downturns also lead to job cuts. No matter how secure employees might think they are in their job, the pink slip could come along at any time. The Toronto Employment Survey 2009 stated that employment was down by 1.4%, a reduction of 18,100 jobs and 1,300 businesses from the previous year, with the manufacturing and retail businesses being hit the hardest. (See Toronto Employment Survey in appendix A.)

We have a different perspective on job security. True security is, in essence, something that cannot be taken away, such as your skills and knowledge. From this, our definition of job security is not a question of being needed by your current company—it's being needed by *any* company that could use you. If you continue your professional development and know how to make yourself hirable at all times, when the time comes, the job hunt is a sure-fire and *reliable* process. This way, you create your own job security. Further to this, when you're not afraid of losing your job, you've reached the nirvana of job security!

Myth: Your first job may not be a reflection of your education

So, you've just graduated from school and you're ready to take on the world by getting a job directly related to your education. Firstly, kudos on your hard work in acquiring that education. Learning should be an on-going process in your life, and the company that hires you will appreciate and recognize this.

You should first ask yourself whether your education complements your goals. Did you find out what you *want* to do in life?

When Connel's parents bought him his first computer, he puked in excitement. From the day that he first switched on that custom-built, 16MB RAM, 333Mhz machine (he's an older Millennial), Connel knew that he would pursue a career in IT after he obtained his bachelor's degree in computer science.

John chose a different path. He first graduated in marketing but didn't find work in this field. Then, going with his gut, he decided to take a couple of information technology courses. John was then hired at an IT retail store and has never looked back since. Today, he is an IT Manager, photographer and public speaker, having successfully combined all three of his interests into his busy life—along with this book.

In the real world, you likely won't find a job that speaks directly to your education—at least, not at first. There are obvious exceptions of course, but don't limit your search to your degree. Many people have managed to get their foot in the door with their first office job. With time and experience, they discovered more about themselves, especially what they truly like to do. If you're fortunate, your company will give you the opportunities you need to change your career path. Or, you can change it yourself. Once you find a job, you will be committing 40 to 50 hours per week (at least) doing that job. Doesn't it make sense to do something that you love, even if it's not directly related to your degree or diploma? Reflect on the things you're good at and start there. Once you land your first job, you can start to work on your path to doing what interests you.

We hope that this overview has enlightened you about what to expect in the real world, and about what's coming up in the following chapters. Now that we've considered and vaulted over the hurdles of misconception, let's get down to finding you that job… ASAP!

CHAPTER 2

THE MILLENNIAL BRAND

Branding is an integral part of a person's professional identity. Considering that the job search process yields results to those who advertise and demonstrate characteristics that make them stand apart from their competitors (other candidates), your brand is an important part of your career development. When discovered and communicated well, your brand can truly distinguish you from the crowd and provide honest insight about what you have to offer the world.

You might be thinking that a brand is commonly something you associate with a commercial product. Well, in a way you are a product on your own, as you have unique skills and abilities that you're 'selling' to other companies so they will hire you. In this sense, you deserve to have a brand of your own and a well-written statement that will attract hiring managers.

Creating a brand statement requires insight into your personality and your experiences. In this chapter, you will uncover what research has shown about how Millennials are branded in the workforce so that you know where your difference and uniqueness lies. Some characteristics may apply to you, others may not, and that's okay. It's all about being unique and discovering what makes you YOU.

The Millennial footprint

Born between 1980 and 2000, you are by far the most tech-savvy generation of all time. You never knew a world without the Internet (maybe some of the older Millennials did). You grew up in a multicultural society where women are finally empowered to be authoritative leaders. Extensive research has been conducted on your generation, and forward-thinking companies are starting to adapt to keeping Millennials (also referred to as Gen Y) engaged in the workplace. Having reviewed these research papers (see appendix B for sources), we would like to share their applicable findings. This review was compelling for us, as older Millennials, to reflect on our own personalities and to decide whether we fit in with the results of the research. For the most part, the results rang true for us.

The biggest difference in the Millennial generation is loyalty to values and purpose. We each have our own values, for example to help others, to save the environment, to advance technology, to take social media to the next level, etc. Whatever the value may be, the research shows that fulfilling our purpose in alignment with our values means more to us than making money. A large percentage of Millennials who participated in the surveys opted to take a lower pay for a job that better aligned with their values. A major cause of concern is that Millennials, when not motivated, tend to leave their jobs at the first available opportunity, ergo the label "Job Hoppers". Our motivation lies in our values and purpose. When we feel that our job doesn't fulfil our purpose, we seek employment elsewhere. We aren't as loyal to companies as the previous generation was. We have lived through economic downturns that have made job security obsolete—and this leads us to question loyalty as a whole.

Millennials also feel that businesses should operate with a high regard for social responsibility. This is undeniably a very positive value, as contributions to our communities will always yield positive outcomes in our society. Millennials want to make a difference in the world, and businesses that strive to do the same will retain Millennial employees.

Millennials also believe in collaboration and teamwork. This is encouraging news for corporations that already realize the added value of reaching goals as teams. However, collaboration in the workplace is not always as easily accomplished as you might think. It requires a culture of managers who are willing to compromise and work with people outside of their own department, and some managers can be territorial about the staff in their area of responsibility.

The entrepreneurial mindset is also prevalent among Millennials. According to the National Society of High School Scholars (NSHSS) 2016 Millennial Career Survey Results, 55 per cent of Millennials report wanting to start their own business. They want to create new ideas and see those ideas come to life and have an impact on the people and world around them. Within an organization, this is called an *intra*preneurial mindset, where employees are given opportunities to bring their ideas to life and thrive on the impact of their initiatives. That sounds like an amazing company to work for, doesn't it? Gmail for example, was an outcome of Google's 20% Time policy, which allowed Google engineers to spend 20 per cent of their work time on their own projects.

So, let's address the elephant in the room—"Millennials are lazy" and referred to as the "Me Me Me Generation". We've even heard the term "codults" (perhaps a reference to the coddling from parents). We are also branded as the "entitled" generation. We've heard these labels many times from our previous generation's blogs and publications, yet *research suggests otherwise.* There is no doubt that Millennials' working styles are different from those of older generations.

We wonder how the Baby Boomers labelled 20-something Gen Xers back in the day. Were they kinder? In truth, negative labels are often applied by 40-somethings to the group in their 20-somethings. Is that realistic? Are you expecting someone who is 20 years your junior to have the same work ethic as you? That, in itself, is the reason why we tend to disregard these labels.

What is perceived as entitled is merely Millennials' ability to question authority. We are not the Yes Sir or Yes Boss generation. We speak our minds and find ways to work smarter rather than harder, using technology to our benefit. Is working smarter to find quicker ways of getting things done being termed as lazy now? Are so many of us trying to become CEOs overnight that we are deemed entitled? There are enough Millennials out there working their ass off who truly represent what our generation is about. The few who are not pulling their weight do not represent our generation as a whole.

Throughout this book, we will be making reference to two types of Millennials, based on Aon Hewitt's Mindset research. Emerging Millennials are Millennials who are just out of college or university and seeking corporate employment for the first time. The challenges they face are different from Established Millennials, who already have their feet wet with three to five years (or more) of experience in the workforce.

The biggest myth of all: "Follow your passion"

We reserved a special spot for this myth, as we felt it deserved attention at a place where you discover your brand and where your career should be headed. There are countless publications out there on the importance of following your dreams, finding your passion, doing that *one* thing.

While we do not want to discredit these words entirely, because we do believe that we all have passions and dreams, it's unwise to limit yourself to pursuing one thing alone.

There are exceptions. Medical students and scientists graduated from university knowing that they would be men and women of science. But the majority of us emerge from college and university either asking ourselves *Now what?* or assuming that we need to find work in the field that we majored in. Let's not forget the sway of our parents and family. According to the NSHSS 2016 Millennial Career Survey, 78 per cent of Millennials reported that their parents influenced their career choices.

The truth is, unless you are as confident as a charging bull about what you want to achieve in your life, *do not* be afraid to experiment with any field that sparks your interest. Author and Millennial supporter Adam "Smiley" Poswolsky, in his book *The Quarter-Life Breakthrough*, advocates finding what interests you by constantly trying new things and using entry-level positions to discover for yourself where your interests lie.

What is passion anyway? Most people associate it with a hobby or a field or an industry. We respectfully disagree. To us, passion is tied into your beliefs and your strengths. You may not know what your beliefs and strengths are yet, but in time you start to discover these for yourself. Steve Jobs was passionate about Zen Buddhism before technology. Condoleezza Rice was a talented classical musician before she started studying politics. One of my favourite questions to ask people—and that always throws them off—is "What causes you to lose track of time (outside of entertainment)?" Give yourself a minute to think of this answer… not as easy as you thought, eh?

When Connel asked himself this question, he pondered over it for an entire week-end. The answer he finally came up with is, "I lose track of time when I explain something I've newly learned to somebody else." This led him to believe that what he values is sharing knowledge with others. He can attach many type of jobs to this belief—he could be trainer, a teacher, a consultant, a coach or a team leader.

And so, if your goal is to find a "dream job" that "follows your passion," we encourage to rethink your strategy, because your ideal job is not as complicated as you think. According to a great article at **8000hours.org**, there are six ingredients to a dream job:

1. Work you're good at
2. Work that helps others
3. Work that engages you and lets you enter a state of flow (freedom, variety, clear tasks, feedback)
4. Supportive colleagues
5. A job that meets your basic needs, such as fair pay, a short commute and reasonable hours
6. A job that fits your personal life

You may have majored in a specific field or industry in college or university, or you may have already had a couple of years of work or volunteer experience in one area. That's great—start there! Also think about the YouTube channels you subscribe to, or newsletters or blogs that you read. Are you learning about something you'd like to pursue from these points of interest? Think about the volunteering and community service that you've done—is there anything in particular that you enjoyed about it?

Don't limit yourself by clinging on to what you presume to be a passion. Just because you own a DSLR camera doesn't mean that your only goal in life is to become a photographer; graphic design may be an alternative option. If what you're currently doing doesn't feel right for you, be willing to try new things, because discovering your passion is a journey of experimenting with many opportunities that *you* pursue.

Discover your strengths and beliefs

Personal branding is a vast subject, and you will find a lot information about it online. To us, it's all about discovering who you uniquely are, what you're good at and how others perceive you. We call that your *beliefs*, your *strengths* and your *impact*.

In this section, we talk about discovering your strengths and beliefs. Your beliefs define *why* you do what you do, so determining what your beliefs really are requires extensive self-reflection. If you are just starting out in your career, think about your past experiences on projects or volunteering opportunities. If you already have a few years of work experience, think about how you operate at your job and working with others.

When Connel asked himself questions to create his own brand, here's what he came up with:

What do I do differently from others? I communicate to my team face to face as often as I can. *Why?* I believe that people, not tools, drive success. And unlike machines, people need to be motivated, guided and given a sense of purpose to do their jobs.

When I'm given a job to do, what's the first thing I do? I find out who else has done it already and learn from their experience. *Why?* I don't like reinventing the wheel. If a task has already been accomplished by someone else, that person is skilled and experienced at doing it. I believe in learning from that person and others, tweaking where necessary.

When doing a task, what considerations do I take? I foresee all angles, consequences, and risks associated with taking on a task. *Why?* I fear failure, so I take calculated risks to minimize the negative impact of a task on people and time.

When dealing with others, what's my approach? I prefer to find common ground to seek win-win situations. *Why?* Because I believe in being fair, and I'm uncomfortable with conflict.

Connel's personal example should provide ideas on how to start this exercise. It's not easy because we don't often take the time to reflect on ourselves. If you take this exercise seriously, we guarantee that you will raise your own self-awareness, and this will be valuable both for your own personal benefit and for creating your brand. Note: Don't just focus on your strengths. Be honest with yourself and think about your weaknesses as well. Don't be afraid to acknowledge your vulnerability because your weaknesses also drive you to make decisions.

Exercise:

Ask yourself the following questions to start thinking about your beliefs:

1. What do I do differently from others? Why?
2. When I'm given a job to do, what's the first thing I do? Why?
3. When doing a task, what considerations do I take? Why?
4. When dealing with others, what's my approach? Why?

Your answers to the *whys* at the end of every question are your beliefs. Your answers to the first part of each question indicate your strengths and reveal *how* you put your beliefs into practice.

The above are just sample questions. By all means, go ahead and create your own questions that allow you to discover *why* and *how* you do what you do.

Everyone has unique strengths that they bring to an organization, and this is why teamwork is so important. Every task or project benefits from a collection of strengths that spawn from the individual beliefs of different people. The individual who values documentation can be in charge of organizing the content of information. The individual who values numbers and calculation can compute the results of the task. The individual who values collaboration can manage communication within the team, and so on.

Discover your impact

Your impact is how you influence others. This is truly a unique and surprisingly fun exercise, because you may be oblivious to how others perceive you. It is also an important aspect of your brand because its ultimate purpose is to attract others who are seeking the strengths and skills that you can offer to them.

You will, of course, have presumptions about what you *think* others see, or perhaps how you *want* others to see you too.

Exercise:

Ask yourself the following questions:

1. Why do people approach me?
2. What are people seeking when they ask for my advice?
3. How do I react when asked for help or advice?
4. How do people feel when they are done talking to me?

Once again, expand on these questions to include these situations:

1. When you had conflicts
2. When you supported somebody
3. When you actively helped others,
   and more.

Whether you're aware of it or not, you have an influence to the people around you. Each person has a unique aura that represents part of his or her brand. We encourage you to ask your friends and co-workers the same questions. You may be surprised by the kinds of answers you receive. This is commonly referred to as *360-degree feedback.*

Here are Connel's answers to these example questions:

Why do people approach me? I smile a lot and I have a reputation for being helpful when I can.

What are people seeking when ask for my advice? Knowledge on technology, how-to's on process-related matters, my thoughts on books they have read and the music industry (one of my hobbies).

How do I react when asked for help or advice? My default reaction is to give it, but I'm always conscious of my time.

How do people feel when they are done talking with me? They feel confident that I've done my best to help. They have direction on what to do next, and clear expectations have been set.

The goal of uncovering your beliefs, strengths and impact is to create a brand statement. We will cover your brand statement as a part of your resumé and LinkedIn Profile in chapter 4.

Emerging Millennials: Where do I start?

You may have just completed graduate school, with limited part-time work experience or volunteer or community work under your belt. You've reflected on this experience and created a list of your beliefs, strengths and impact. Of course, you must also consider what you majored in. You might be working a survival job at the moment to make ends meet and pay off a student loan. If this is what you are doing right now, there is untapped potential in you that only *you* can bring to the corporate world.

You must now decide on a career path, and you're tempted to believe that what you majored in is the best choice available. But you might be unsure. Our advice? Don't sweat the small stuff. It's important to get your feet wet and jump into the work environment as soon as possible. Your career is a path of self-discovery and experimentation that will be paved with opportunities and guided by your willingness to grab those opportunities, or better yet create them on your own.

John has also been in the IT field his entire career, starting off selling computers at a retail store, and now managing an IT Service Desk. But while also authoring this book, he has pursued public speaking, photography and sharing knowledge in leadership and team building.

Connel started off his career in Information Technology, because he knew for certain that was where he wanted to be. He majored in computer science in grad school and has held IT positions ever since. But right now, by authoring a book he's educating Millennials on how to be selected for job interviews. During his career, he realized his strength is not in technology, but in helping others by sharing knowledge. It took him 13 years to figure that out!

Our personal experiences provide ample evidence that overthinking your first step is a waste of time. Inevitably, your career will be controlled by unforeseen and unknown opportunities that present themselves along the way. If you need further proof of the power of these opportunities, consider the stepping stones in the career path of legends of our time. Check out the cool infographics of about Steve Jobs, Mark Zuckerberg and Elon Musk at **fundersandfounders.com**.

So, pick a field—possibly the one you majored in—and see where it takes you. If you're uncertain that your major is where you want to go, you can always take on volunteering opportunities in another field that may interest you. Once you've selected your field, the next step is to discover your target job title that will help you in your search for work. We will cover your target job title in the next chapter.

Established Millennials: Am I on the right track?

If you are a Millennial with several years of work experience under your belt, you may be considering whether it's time to move on to something else. Maybe you picked your so-called field of interest after succumbing to the pressures of finding work to pay the bills, or the decision to comply with your graduate school major, or the power of parental pressure. If you are in a job situation that isn't working for you, it's never too late to make a change. In its entirety, this book will show that your career journey depends on you—and lies in you developing yourself to be hir-able by many companies. You alone will create your own job security.

Does what you're doing now serve your purpose? Be careful to differ-entiate between your field of work and your manager or company. You may be in the right field, but with the wrong company and surrounded by the wrong people. Remember that it's impossible to find 100 per cent gratification from any job, because every job has elements that you dis-like.

> Connel *hates* mundane work, but he knows that doing quality scoring and timesheet approvals is part of his job description. The opportunities he is given to lead his team far outweigh the few hours a month he has to devote to mundane work.

Do you still feel that it's time for a change? Then it's time to roll up your sleeves and make that change happen. It's certainly not going to happen if you sit around and wait for it to come your way. We realize the diffi-culties of working eight hours each day while looking for work at the same time. As we stated before, job searching can be a job on its own, so it should feel as though you are working two jobs. But always remem-ber that you're at an advantage—when you're employed, you appear more attractive to hiring managers, especially if you currently work in a reputable organization. Our advice: Always aim to *monkey swing* your way to a new job—let go of the previous tree branch only once you have a firm grip on the next one.

Takeaways and exercises

We uncovered what makes Millennials different and how the world sees you. We introduced the concept of your brand and its importance—we'll come back to that when we talk about your resumé and LinkedIn profile. We stated that your brand is a compilation of your beliefs, strengths and impact, and how you can discover each of these elements. We also talked about the two types of Millennials that will benefit from this book, *emerging* and *established*.

We also talked about the hazards of clinging on to the hopes of finding a dream job and your one true passion. Your passion is what results from *purpose* and *values*. You may not have discovered these fully yet, so to delay your quest for work in order to nail down a perfect job is a waste of time and opportunity.

Exercise:

Reflect on your past and experience and start discovering your beliefs, strengths and impact. Note them down on your phone or tablet for safekeeping. You will need your list for later exercises when we create your resumé and LinkedIn profile.

Coming up is a chapter that's especially geared to emerging Millennials who are still on the path to discovering where to start.

CHAPTER 3

CHOOSE YOUR COMPANY

Now that you've reflected on your past experiences as well as the unique beliefs and strengths that you bring to our world, it's time to choose where and how you can utilize your talents.

The company you choose to work for is critical to your success. Every company has its own distinct values and culture, and it is important to be part of a company with values and culture that align with yours. You may be a good fit in some companies, but not so much in others. Although there are online resources that give you some insight into a company's culture, only you are the best judge of which company or companies are right for you.

If you're just starting your career, we encourage you not to spend too much time dwelling on finding your perfect company. Sure, we'd all like to work for Google and Facebook, but cast your net wide because you can discover your purpose at many organizations.

This chapter serves as a high-level guide to important considerations when you are drawing up a list of the companies you want to apply to work for. Yes, it *is* a choice.

Scouting for companies

You may be thinking *I'll work for any company. I just need a job right now so I can pay off my student debt,* or you may be thinking *Google is the only company I'd want to work for*—two vastly different points of view. Depending on your situation, you decide how high you want to set the bar. Just how picky do you want to be?

> When Connel first moved to Canada, as desperate as any new immigrant husband and father would be, he had a take-what-you-get mindset. Fortunately, he found himself working at one of the largest enterprises in Canada whose values in innovation, employee development and customer service aligned with his own. Now, his views have changed. If he were to ever change jobs, he'd be a lot pickier because he can afford to be. Similarly, when his wife is relieved of the early years of motherhood and is ready to join the workforce again, she will be picky as well because they can survive on his income alone.

It really depends on your personal circumstances. If you have urgent loans to pay off or a family to support, you may decide to broaden your job search horizon. If you have a steady income and some momentum in a promising career, instead you'll target those companies that would be lucky to have you.

Every company has a different culture and values, and employees feel the effects of these every day in the workplace. Your decision about the company you select should depend on whether those cultures and values align with yours. Research shows that Millennials strongly feel that every organization should serve its community. While most large enterprises are engaged in community activities, don't expect start-ups to be there yet. A company may not check off all the boxes on your values list, so it's essential to prioritize those values.

So how do you know what a company's culture is like or what corporate beliefs are present before you start working there? The most popular site that's well known for its dedication to employee opinion is **glassdoor.com**. Now well established, this site and its statistics are referenced by several blogs and posts that we've read. Employees are allowed to anonymously post their opinion about their companies at Glassdoor, so you can read personal reviews of what it's like to work for an organization. But read them with a grain of salt. As with all reviews, there are bound to be negative and cynical commenters who find nasty things to say about everything.

You can also Google the company's values and see what comes up. Every company has a publicly visible mission statement that describes the organization's purpose and beliefs. If you type "*XYZ company*'s values and beliefs" into Google, you will most likely end up at the company's website where you can read that mission statement. We're not saying that you choose a company *exclusively* on its values, for these reasons:

1. There's no guarantee that the company really operates by those values today.
2. You may not know what your own values are at the moment.
3. You can't know for certain whether there is any link between company's stated values and its culture or people—which are just as important.

Use a company's values and mission statement purely as a guideline. In those situations where you have two job offers and you're trying to decide which company to choose, the mission statement, values and beliefs of a company may be the deciding factor. (We hope that you will find yourself in such a fruitful predicament by the end of this book!)

So now that you're aware of how to find the values, beliefs and culture of companies, let's look at them from the perspective of size.

Working for start-ups

With the Millennial generation having more of an entrepreneurial mindset, it's no surprise to see a lot of start-up companies taking root in the business world. According to **Toronto.ca**, statistics show that in 2016, 36.2 per cent of Toronto's companies had been in business for less than five years. Start-ups are commonly associated with technology, but can be anything from a small restaurant to a software development company, and can have anywhere from a few to a hundred employees. According to Innovation, Science and Economic Development Canada (**ic.gc.ca**), as of December 2015, a whopping 97.9 per cent of employers in Canada were small businesses. It's no surprise that in the same year, 70.5 per cent of Canadian jobs filled were in small businesses, thus proving that these small businesses (commonly known as SMEs) play a vital role in employing Canadians across the country.

There are several upsides to working at a start-up:

You are in close contact with the big players of the company. Many employee ideas and suggestions are implemented, affecting a large percentage of the organization, which is deeply fulfilling.

There is less bureaucracy in small companies, so your influence goes a longer way, and you receive higher levels of appreciation for your work. There is comparatively less (but always some) office politics. You can get in direct contact with key decision-makers if politics starts to impede your decision-making.

One of the biggest upsides we see with successful smaller companies is the potential for promotion. If the company grows, you grow with it, most likely because your ideas, hard work and effort were easily recognized. If the company eventually transforms to a medium or large organization, you may find yourself sitting high up the organization chart, promoted there because of your lasting experience in the company.

> When Connel joined a small organization in the medical services industry, there were no more than 40 employees in the office. In four years, that company grew to 300 employees, and he was promoted twice along the way.

The small business environment is definitely fast paced. Decisions are made quickly, with less red tape, because owners are more focused on getting off the ground and growing their business quickly. Everything—from the interview process to authorizing expansion projects—happens relatively quickly.

But there are downsides to working within a start-up too. The biggest disadvantage, of course, is risk. There is an undeniable possibility that a start-up could fail before it picks up enough momentum to achieve the next level. We're not saying that large enterprises don't fail, but statistically speaking, start-ups have a higher chance of not making it to four years. According to **ic.gc.ca**, in 2013 the total number of SME 'births' was 78,430, compared with 83,240 'deaths'—resulting in a net decrease of 4,810 businesses.

You may also find less focus on industry standards and best practices in smaller organizations. Processes and procedures aren't as streamlined, and a lot of manual effort is required to get things done. Because automation is expensive, owners are not willing to spend money on automating operations until they have made a successful start in the marketplace with their products. Don't expect to be filling expense reports in some fancy enterprise resource planning (ERP) system any time soon. Overall, budgets are generally tighter for business support-related needs over revenue-generating needs.

Smaller teams provide only limited room and fewer opportunities for parallel growth. The organization won't have many openings available internally to which you can apply. And due to the smaller size, you may find yourself a one-person show doing it all. That's not necessarily a bad thing, mind you, as doing it all allows you to diversify your experience. For those looking to hone their expertise on a very specific skill set, however, a start-up may not give you that chance. The organization expects you to multi-task and do it all.

Compared to larger companies, start-ups may not have as many attractive benefits, including a wealth accumulation program, private medical and life insurance, paid training programs, pension plans, etc. If you're looking for an organization to sponsor these perks for you as part of your total rewards, you're most likely to find it in mid- to large-sized businesses.

Working for large enterprises

If you opt to work for a large enterprise organization, there are lots of benefits and considerations. You'll find plenty of openings for these companies from job search websites, and they most likely have their own careers section on their web site. Large enterprise organizations well exceed the 1,000-employee mark and provide opportunities for you to gain valuable experience.

Some of the key benefits of working for a large enterprise company are:

Working environments are more advanced and professional. Most likely, the company has invested in extensive technology to manage and automate daily operations, which can be effective at engaging Millennials.

Simple tasks don't require multiple sheets of manual paperwork, thus allowing employees to remain focused on mindful work.

Large team environments provide an excellent workplace for Millennials seeking to work collaboratively with peers. Projects are usually on a larger scale, and exposure to this kind of experience is extremely valuable for your future.

Large enterprises may have also modernized facilities. Creating modern workspaces, areas for entertainment, facilities such as gyms, and other wellness programs can provide highly effective stress relief for hard-working Millennials.

Learning and development programs also go a long way in a large company that has matured to a state where there is a budget for creating training programs for its staff. The organization we currently work at has a learning and development portal with thousands of online training courses available at no cost to the employee.

Working for large well-known organizations undoubtedly does wonders for your credibility as a working employee. Hiring managers are impressed when they see you've been trusted to work for a prestigious well-known organization.

When it comes to benefits, in addition to health and wealth programs and insurance, large organizations extend their influence to other companies as well, offering employee discount programs—discounted rates on certain products and services from other companies such as banks or insurance companies.

However, there are some downsides as well. While the glitz and glamour of working for a well-known enterprise organization is impressive, you need to be aware of certain pitfalls you may encounter in their vast environments.

Because there is so much more bureaucracy and red tape to go through, change takes a long time—a *very long time*. This can be frustrating for those trying to quickly create a positive change in the organization.

It's definitely not an environment where everyone knows your name. Our current organization has 30,000 employees, and we barely know anyone beyond our own team. This distance creates frustration when managing operations as well. If you're trying to figure out who to contact to accomplish a particular task, tracking down the right person can be like finding the proverbial needle in a haystack. It's only after prolonged tenure that this gap can be reasonably closed.

Unlike in smaller organizations, unless you're closer to the top of the corporate ladder, the stories of your successes will almost never reach the ears of the top brass. You have to celebrate your victories within your team and you may find that *you* have to pat yourself on the back for a job well done.

Competition for internal moves is also stiff, simply because there are many people applying for the same position. So, while the opportunities are plentiful, you have to work harder to beat out the competition.

Working for mid-sized companies

Mid-size companies are making the transition from start-ups to large enterprise and could have anywhere between 100 and 1,000 employees. Companies in this size group possess a mix of the features (both pros and cons) discussed above, and at varying levels. The biggest advantage of working in a mid-size company is that it has reached a certain level of security, so the risks associated with start-up businesses are significantly reduced. The company's product is well on the way to achieving success, and the organization is still growing. It's still not too late to hop on board the success bandwagon and catch that wave of growth with this organization.

The organization will, however, experience growing pains at this stage, and will start to invest in affordable means of automation and technology as it tries to beat the competition and transform into a large enterprise. These are critical times during which the company needs loyal and committed employees to get it to where it needs to go.

Make your choices

The above descriptions are opinions of the authors of *Zero2Hired*, based on our collective experience in the workforce. By no means should you take these pros and cons as blanket rules for all organizations. There is no right or wrong involved in your choice of company type that you choose to work for. Using the information sections on small, medium and large businesses as a guide, scout for the companies that you feel resonate with your values at this point in time. Don't get hung up on finding the *perfect* answer. No company will be perfect, and no job will be perfect either. As long as the job allows you to fulfil most of the beliefs and strengths that are important to you, it's a good fit.

It's a fair point to note that hiring managers give preference to people who have worked in companies similarly sized to their own. If you've worked for a large enterprise, you may already have experience working with automation and technology tools such as SharePoint, Oracle, and SAP.

If you narrow down a list of companies that you would really like to work for, create Google Alerts about those companies so that you will receive notification every time there are new developments. This information could be vital later in the job hunt process, as you will soon see.

Contract and full-time work

You may be considering which is the best option to take. Many companies offer both types of positions, so let's talk about this—both from your point of view and the company's—so that you have a thorough understanding before you decide what types of positions you want to target.

Contract positions are becoming more and more popular with organizations. As you can imagine, there is a cost-benefit reason for this to be happening. As of December 2016, of the 18.2 million full-time employed people in Canada's workforce, approximately 2.8 million were self-employed. Contract positions may put more money into your pocket, but to the organization, it's definitely a cheaper solution. In contract positions, you won't be paid if you don't work for any reason. Whereas in a full-time position, you will be entitled to paid vacation as well as paid sick days.

As a 'contractor', you don't necessarily have a designated reporting manager, although you still answer to someone. You will always report to a full-time manager who is overseeing your efforts. If you're not performing up to the mark, your contract can be terminated at any time. In this sense, contract jobs have a higher risk of insecurity.

For full-time positions, Canadian laws prevent wrongful terminations, thus requiring organizations to go through several Human Resources (HR) department-approved procedures before you can be let go. In this sense, there is more security in a full-time role. We're not saying that you're employed for life, as different circumstances could arise—such as your position being made redundant—that could also lead to you losing your job. But compared to a contract, a full-time position is far more secure. You'd need to research on employee protection laws in your own province/country to understand how secure full-time positions are.

Most U.S. states, for example, presume 'At-will employment', where the employer is entitled to fire you for any arbitrary reason, and you have limited legal rights to fight your termination.

As a full-time employee, you are also entitled to receive all the benefits that the company has to offer, such as paid leave, employee discounts, life and health insurance, and other perks and benefits. If you are a contractor, you are responsible for taking care of those life details on your own and at your own expense. This is another reason why it's better for the bottom line for a company to hire contractors.

In our experience, most people opt for the security of a full-time position. In fact, according to the Deloitte Millennial Survey, two-thirds of Millennials choose the security and fixed-income of full-time employment. But we have come across individuals who prefer a contractor's title in order to put more money into their pockets and take advantages of tax benefits associated with contract work. It's really up to you—there are pros and cons to both options. If you are an emerging Millennial, don't limit yourself to only seeking full-time positions. If a contract position is within your grasp, go for it! You'll gain valuable experience that will help to beef up your resumé. And you never know, that contract position may be converted to full-time if the company really likes you. We both have experience with this situation in our current organization.

Your target job title

Before we move to the next chapter, one of the prerequisites is to determine your target job title. This is the job title that you will typically search for on your favourite job sites and direct your resumé toward. Established Millennials, if you decide to continue down your existing career path, you may already have a title in mind—unless you are considering a career change. Emerging Millennials, if you're just out of school, you may be thinking about your options.

We hope that you've reflected on your values, beliefs and strengths from chapter 2, and have seriously considered what you want to do. The first step is to select a field that you want to start with: let's say it's IT. You might even be more specific if you've majored in this field, so it might be software development or networking. Next, you might type "entry level positions for *[job title]*" into Google and see what comes up. Established Millennials may Google "mid-level positions for…"; the results show the various positions that could fit your search. Again, we want to remind you not to waste your time looking for the "perfect job". This isn't going to happen overnight. Your career will always be about experimentation and it's going to last over 40 years, so you have the time!

You may still be uncertain about whether you're selecting the right job title. Visit the website **onetonline.org**, which offers a skills-based approach to searching for job titles. If you've already found a job title of interest, you can use this site to validate the skills required for the position. A search for the target job title on your favourite job search sites will reveal typical requirements for that job. From that, you can see if it's what you're looking for.

The most effective approach is speaking to someone already in the field you want to pursue. There's nothing like getting real-world, hands-on knowledge from an experienced practitioner (maybe a relative, friend, or a friend of a friend) in that field. We call these discussions 'informational interviews' and will discuss them later in more detail.

At the very least, you can seek the advice of a career counsellor from your postsecondary school who can also help you with finding a target job title that's a right fit for you. It's okay to seek a professional's help if you're struggling to get off the ground, but remember that *you* are the only person who will know which is the right job for you. No matter what job you do, there is *always* something to learn from it that will benefit your career. There is no such thing as the wrong job.

> John's first job involved driving a truck and running a crew of two people doing lawn care and landscaping. On this job, he learned how to give people instructions, manage work schedules and speak to customers. He then moved on to a retail job selling computers, and was eventually employed at one of the largest enterprises in Canada.

You don't have to lock down one specific job title. If there is a range of jobs that interest you, by all means, keep track and pursue all of them. It will improve the chances of you finding your next job, but it will also mean more prep work. That's coming up in the next chapter.

Takeaways and exercises

So, we have now covered the fact that different companies have unique cultures and values and the importance of finding the right company (although not the perfect one) that aligns with your own values.

We also noted our opinions of the pros and cons of working for start-ups, medium and large organizations, in either a full-time or contract role. There is no right or wrong for any of these choices—it's really up to your personal situation and preferences.

Finally, we addressed knowing your target job title or titles, based on the kind of job that you want to do. If you're just starting out, you can select a title based on your own preferences, or you can Google your answer, or seek professional help on it.

Exercise:

Drawing on what you have learned in this chapter, make the following notes:

1. The various target job titles that you want to pursue in your job hunt
2. The types of companies you'd want to work for
3. Any specific target companies you have in mind. Also check online to see whether their culture and values align with your own

CHAPTER 4

THE CONVERSATIONAL RESUMÉ

Now that you know your target job title and the types of companies where you can see yourself working, it's time to make sure you have everything you need before you begin your job search. We know that you're itching to dive straight into applying for jobs, but trust us, the last thing you'd want is to allow an opportunity to pass you by because you were unknowingly *unprepared*. Imagine if you went ahead and applied for a job and then you received a call the next day. Everything is going well until the caller asks you for the name of a reference—and you don't have one! Epic fail! The person who will be hired is the one who is the most prepared for the interview (telephone or otherwise). *Never undervalue or underestimate the importance of being appropriately prepared.*

So remember, as eager as you may be to start applying for jobs, you take a huge risk on every job application you pursue without being prepared. Bite the bullet and apply the knowledge you will gain from the next two chapters, and we promise you—the time you spend job hunting will be substantially reduced. You only get one shot at every interview, so be prepared!

Connel once thought he was thoroughly prepared for an interview because he had researched everything under the sun about the company itself. He thought that he would know more about the company than the interviewer! Having dug up so much detail about that organization, Connel went to the interview totally psyched by his impressive, in-depth knowledge of their products and current projects. As it turns out, he was only asked one question relating to his knowledge of the company. For the rest of the interview, he was grilled about his weaknesses, asked to recall when things had gone wrong, questioned about when he had last made a mistake, asked how he would manage a tough employee, and forced to field an assortment of curveball questions. Although Connel did manage to answer every question, he fumbled through most of them, taking a minute or two to come up with the answer. Clearly, he was unprepared. As you can imagine, Connel left that interview feeling really low—he had messed up a great opportunity. He also realized his mistake right away—he had been so focused on doing his homework about the company that he had forgotten to do the homework about himself!

A tip on staying motivated

Preparing yourself for the job hunt takes time and effort, and you may feel that it's unfulfilling because you're not actually applying for jobs yet. Let's face it, most people don't have the patience to plan and prepare— they just want to dive right in—so this period may present a challenge to your motivation. Our advice is to find an 'accountability partner' or a coach, someone who is willing to touch base with you on a regular basis to check on your progress. Ideally, this person should not be too close to you (such as a close family member or friend), because you can easily brush them off. Someone who is an *acquaintance* would be better suited for the role. Having an accountability partner has been proven to result in higher commitment levels. Knowing that this person is going to call or text you in three days to ask if you completed a task will motivate you to actually do it.

Your unique resumé and cover letter

Let's start from the top. The age-old practice of using a resumé (also known as a *curriculum vitae* or CV) as a documented introduction to what you have to offer a company is still very much alive today. The best way to describe a resumé is as *a marketing document for the product that is you*. It showcases your brand to the target audience and is intended to sell you to them.

Let's remember one thing: the purpose of the resumé is to open the door to the interview. That is all. It does *not* guarantee the job. Obtaining the interview is, of course, half the battle. While the practice of selling yourself with a resumé still exists, you are in control of its content, and the content will make you stand out.

This book is not going to tell you how to write a resumé and letter in the traditional sense. That very word 'traditional' means everybody has and is still doing it. Everybody is *not* who this book wants you to be. If you aim to stand out from the crowd, doesn't it make sense that your resumé should do the same? We are, therefore, going to help you to create a resumé that is different—and very much unique to you.

First, we will do away with resumé jargon such as 'self-motivated' or 'fast learner' or 'passionate'. When the hiring manager goes through 50 resumés, 49 of them will have this lame and tiresome terminology. In contrast, *your* resumé will tell a *unique story* of *what you do*. That hiring manager is going to remember you!

Moreover, this approach will make writing your resumé fun (believe it or not). We hope that you will come away from this exercise saying to yourself, *I can actually see myself in my resumé*. Resumé writing is both an art and a skill. If you're not comfortable with writing, now's the time to sharpen those skills. A well-written resumé will demonstrate to the employer that you have written communication skills—a *must* in today's email-dominated office environments.

Why won't a traditional resumé work?

Very simple, because everybody is doing it. The purpose of your resumé is to land you an interview, and interviews are almost guaranteed to those who *stand out*. Everyone claims to be professional and passionate and driven, but we definitely can't call 49 people for interviews. A traditional resumé may contain a statement such as this:

> "I am a highly adaptable, motivated, fast learner with exceptional organizational skills."

A hiring manager would wonder how anyone reading this could know whether you, in fact, are adaptable and a fast learner: "What's your perception of adaptation and learning? Did it take you eight months to adapt to your environment and learn the ropes of your last job, and do you call that fast? That's far too long in my book. We need someone who can learn the job in two months. Oh, and you say that you've got exceptional organizational skills. What's so exceptional about them? What do you do from an organizing perspective that most people cannot do? Let me read the rest of your resumé to see if you've explained how. Oh wait, you haven't. So now what? Are we just supposed to blindly trust you even though we've never met?"

Moving on to experience, you might find something like:

> "Reviewed requirements and expectations for new products and designs."

And once again, from the hiring manager's perspective: "Okay, it's great to review requirements and expectations, but *why* did you do it? *Who* did it benefit? It doesn't state that you created those requirements and expectations. It just says that you reviewed them. Did you actually *change anything* or were you just passing your time by reading a document when you didn't have to?"

You see where we're going with this.

Why won't a traditional cover letter work?

The cover letter is the introduction to your resumé. Its purpose is to stimulate the reader's interest in reading your resumé. Your cover letter will, whether you intend it to or not, create a perception in the reader's mind of what to expect in your resumé.

If you're cover letter sounds the same as everyone else's: "Dear Sir / Madam" ***yawn*** "I was interested in the job posting you had for" ***yawn*** "an HR assistant. I am a hardworking, self-motivated professional" ***yawn*** "looking to further my career." ***ok, we're done here*** You've already created a negative perception in the reader's mind, and that person might just glance over your resumé for five seconds as a formality and toss it.

We've read blogs from professional recruiters who report that if the cover letter starts with a 'Dear Sir/Madam' or 'To whom it may concern', they don't even bother reading the rest!

There's a reason why school gave you homework. It's because in the real world, people appreciate folks who do their homework, and the cover letter is where you show that you've done it. If your letter sounds like it's the same template copied and pasted from other job applications, that's not a demonstration of you doing your homework. But if personalized references are geared to the person you're writing to, the company, and the job, *that* reveals a prepared individual who has already demonstrated a level of commitment.

The recruiter and the hiring manager

Before we delve in to constructing your brand-new marketing document that's going to stand out from the crowd, as with all marketing strategies, it's wise to know who your target audience is.

In the world of hiring, there are four key players in the game. First, there's *you*, the brand you're promoting to land your next job. Next there's the *competition*, who you're trying to beat and from whom you need to stand apart. Then there are the two key players who have the authority to hand you the job—the *recruiter* and the *hiring manager*.

Both the recruiter and the hiring manager have a common goal—they are trying to fill a vacant position. There are, however, notable differences between the two, as shown in the following table:

Difference	Recruiter	Hiring Manager
Authority	Authorized to short-list and screen applicants for an advertised job.	Authorized to give the job to an applicant, in the case of both advertised and non-advertised jobs.
Responsibility	Dedicated to the hiring process.	Dedicated to other responsibilities; hiring is an additional task
Hiring requirements	Seeks candidates who match the skills and qualifications negotiated with the hiring manager for the job.	Seeks candidates who have the competency and soft skills to do the job and fit in with the team and environment? (In addition to the posted skills and qualifications).
Awareness	Only aware of the advertised jobs.	Aware of advertised and unadvertised future jobs.

These differences are far from subtle, and each plays a vital role that affects your job search strategy. Common sense would dictate that you keep your efforts focused on the hiring manager. After all, that is the person with the authority to actually hire you and the one who is also aware of upcoming positions in the organization's hidden job market.

But keeping recruiters completely in the dark would be a mistake too. Even though they are only aware of the advertised market, their awareness spans multiple departments and companies, whereas a hiring manager is only aware of opportunities in his or her own department or division.

Recruiters are not subject matter experts in the field for which they are hiring, yet they are responsible for ensuring that the hiring process is followed, especially from a legal standpoint. Among other things, recruiters ensure that employers are compliant with laws and regulations to ensure that recruitment practices are fair and non-discriminatory. When a hiring manager and recruiter meet to discuss the requirements of a new job to post, the hiring manager calls the shots on what's needed for the job. The recruiter may provide some guidelines on what's required to conform to company and industry standards and policies. The hiring manager is now constrained to limit the details of this job posting to bullet point requirements. And although this manager can visualize the ideal candidate, writing a description of that person is far more challenging. So, a job description's requirements are listed in bullet form, together with an educational requirement and some number of years of experience.

If you remember from chapter 1, this is our list of must-haves and nice-to-haves. Is the hiring manager willing to be flexible? Absolutely. However, from the recruiter's perspective, the requirements are black and white. What was discussed is what we're going to look for. This recruiter will now advertise the job and scour hundreds of applications trying to find the right match to satisfy the hiring manager. The resumés will be searched for the bullet points resulting from the discussion. This is why it is well known that recruiters take six to 10 seconds to scan a resumé. For this reason, they don't much care for paragraphs in a resumé. Because the hiring manager's requirement were in bullet points, the recruiter will recursively scan through the piles of resumés as quickly as possible to just catch those bulleted requirements, along with the *keywords* used in the job description.

The lesson here is that recruiters read resumés very differently from the way hiring managers do. Because there are so many resumés to go through, recruiters prefer a format that contains quick and easy-to-scan bullet points. These reviewers don't care much for uniqueness. Think of these resumés coming at them on an assembly line conveyor belt. Anything that's a 'defect' is ignored. A resumé that stands out and is formatted differently would actually annoy them, just like a defective product on an assembly line. Recruiters don't appreciate brand statements and soft skill explanations—all they want to know is whether the words used on a standard resumé match the bulleted points in the job description.

Hiring managers, however, are different. Because they are the ones who will inevitably end up with the hired candidate, they want someone who is different. They don't just want someone who can do the tasks listed on a job description. They want something more, someone who has the competence to go above and beyond what is asked. Hiring managers would appreciate a unique resumé as well as your personality that shines through from the stories in it.

By contrast, if you want to capture the recruiter's attention on a unique resumé, you must catch that person outside of assembly line mode. The online job application system is the start of the dreaded assembly line process. If you can find an alternate way to access the recruiter, you may be able grab his or her attention with your unique resumé as well. We'll touch more on the delivery process of your resumé in chapter 6.

The conversational resumé

Let us introduce you to a resumé that does capture attention. We call it the 'conversational resumé'.

The conversational resumé is unique because it does away with the same-old-lame-old resumé jargon that reviewers are tired of seeing—passionate, motivated, collaborate, fast learner… You don't use these words in conversation, and neither does the person reading your resumé. These words don't resonate with people anymore, except for the traditionalists. Moreover, since your competition is still afraid of change and sticking with the traditional style of resumé writing, you will definitely stand out in the crowd.

The conversational resumé is also unique because it allows you to tell stories. Instead of listing your experiences and skills in bullet points, you create a story behind each of them. The beauty of stories is that you just state the facts of your experience, and let the readers draw their own conclusions. That resulting thought pattern sticks better in their minds.

Here is an example.

Remember this traditional style job experience in the previous section:

> Reviewed requirements and expectations for new products and designs.

A conversational resumé could present the same point this way:

> "Once the development team completed the functional requirement specification (FRS) document for new modules, I received an email copy to review first, before it was submitted to management. I determined whether the new module would negatively impact our operations, highlighted any risks that I

observed, and performed a cross-check to verify that the costs were in line with our budget. This saved management the time and trouble of communicating back and forth with the development team on any discrepancies."

Now doesn't that have much more impact to the reader? Your conversational resumé should tell a story to the reader about what you do—similar to the way an actual conversation would sound! Stories resonate better with people. This methodology is used in books and speeches and it has now gained its place in resumés.

What about the length of your resumé? The standard size has become two pages. This is acceptable, but we encourage you to stick to a one-pager, especially for entry-level to mid-level roles, which is the target of most Millennials. After over a decade of work experience, Connel's resumé is still one page.

There's a solid reason why we opt for this approach. By now, most of you know how long it takes for a reader to scan a resumé before deciding whether it goes to the interview pile or the junk pile—anywhere from six to 10 seconds. In such a short time frame, and with the tired mind of the hiring manager having such a short attention span, wouldn't a one-pager be enough? Condensed and customized specifically to the job description, of course. *But what about the rest of my experience?* you must be asking yourself. You don't want all the juicy details of your work to go unnoticed, and that's where LinkedIn or your online resumé page comes in. If your one-page resumé has captured the reader's attention, he or she will likely look for more details on your site, or even better, call you for an interview. Once again, remember: *the purpose of the resumé is not to explain what you can do in detail.* It's to get your foot in the door and stimulate the curiosity of the reader just enough to make that person want to call you or meet you in person. Once that happens, your resumé has served its purpose.

If you're still concerned about the condensed one-pager, think of it this way: 80 per cent of your job is operational and boring to the hiring manager. You don't want to focus on that 80 per cent because that's likely what others in the same role as you are putting on their resumé (because they have done the same type of job). Focus on the 20 per cent when you did something unique in that role. With that mindset, we're sure that you can create a condensed one-pager with greater impact than a traditional resumé. If your role was as a telephone receptionist, don't tell them about the 80 per cent of the phone calls. Instead, remember the 20 per cent that were different and create a story about that part of your work.

The solution letter

Conventional cover letters are obsolete. Although a letter is still required to introduce your resumé, the conventional cover letter no longer holds the attention of readers. An effective letter to introduce your resumé should be thought of as a 'solution letter', because you need to introduce yourself as someone who is going to be a solution to a problem.

Here's an important perspective about your job. Every job exists because there is a problem that needs to be solved. From the CEO's perspective, departments exist because of specific problems within the company that need a solution. Finance exists because the money needs to be managed. Sales and marketing exist because someone has to make the product known and then sell it. IT exists because technology is needed to operate a business. From the hiring manager's perspective, inside a specific department the problem is usually an operational activity that he or she does not have the time or the expertise to do. And that's where you come in.

What does this have to do with your letter? You must explain how *you* are the solution to the problem that the hiring manager is facing. You do this by highlighting a specific problem, bringing it front and centre to the hiring manager's mind (so he or she recalls how big the annoyance is), and then stating how *you* can solve it.

The letter is also an opportunity to demonstrate to the hiring manager that you've done your homework—always a plus point. There are three rules to the solution letter:

1. Get personal
2. Get personal
3. Get personal

The solution letter cannot, in any form or shape, sound as thought it's been copied and pasted from a standard template. Addressing the person by name is a minimum requirement. Get personal about the company by researching what's been happening in the news and investigating the products it creates and its values. This is where the Google alerts we suggested setting up earlier would help. Get personal about the hiring manager himself or herself by scoping that person's LinkedIn profile and seeing if there are any awards or experience that you can relate to, and finally, get personal about the job itself and how you will be the solution to the hiring manager's problem.

Important note: When we dig up information about a person, we reference only public-facing, online content for which that individual's intent is clearly for the public to see. In addition to that person's LinkedIn profile, public-facing content can include that person's blogs, news articles (written by or about him/her), etc. Any comments about that person's vacation or family from photos on their Facebook profile would be completely *out of line*.

We will construct a solution letter later in this chapter.

Constructing your conversational resumé

As promised, this is going to be a fun exercise. You may think that resumé writing is specialized skill, what with all the "professional" resumé writers out there. As hiring managers ourselves (and we're pretty sure we speak on behalf of most of the hiring managers out there), we don't care that you've used fancy corporate jargon or that you are a professional who's driven and a fast learner. All we want to know is what you've done in the past or what you're currently doing that will *prove* to us that you have the potential to do the job we have available. If you just *tell* us you're driven or a professional, it's not going to mean squat! Tell us a story that proves it—because that's what we will be doing in the interview. Let this resumé in front of us be a brochure for that event.

First off, remember that we are aiming to limit the resumé to just one page. If you must have a second page, that's okay too. Perhaps your role requires highlighting past projects and in-depth technical qualifications. If this is the case, the second page will be dedicated to those details. *But the first page speaks **only** to what's in the job description.* If you've captured the heart of the hiring manager on the first page, he or she will be curious enough to turn to the second page.

For those trying to stick to one page, remember that your LinkedIn profile or online resumé will provide more details.

Your resumé's layout

There is an abundance of layouts available on the web, and there is no one correct layout. Our suggestion is to pick one that you like and work with it. The resumé template that we have created seems to be attracting a lot of attention, and people seem to appreciate its format, so we'd like to share it with you.

The resumé has six sections:

1. A header containing your name and various contact details
2. An executive summary containing your brand statement — why, how and what you are
3. Your soft skills and your innate abilities
4. Your professional experience: the stories of your past responsibilities
5. Your qualifications and any additional certifications that you hold
6. Your education: your highest diploma or degree

You can find a free copy of the layout at our website:

http://www.zero2hired.com/resources

In the template, you will see that each section contains a brief description of what that section is about, and now we're going to elaborate on each.

The Header

The header starts off with your name. Below that is the job title of the position you are applying for. Note: Based on the job description, you will customize every resumé before you send it out, so you must modify the job title to *match the job title of the advertised position.* You may ask *What about the resumés that I'll send for unadvertised positions in the hidden job market?* In the previous chapter, you decided on your target job title. That's what would go here. (Different companies have title variations for what is essentially the same type of job, so you can pick the most common title you've analyzed through your research and experience and use that.)

Below the job title is your address, which is very important. Commuting is an important aspect of your work life, and if the reviewers notice that it will take you four hours to get to work, they may choose to discard your resumé. Applying for this position may be a waste of your time and theirs. The exception of course, is if you explicitly state you're willing or planning to relocate in your solution letter.

Your phone contact must be a cellphone, no questions asked, and it's important to advertise a means of communication by which you can be reached at any time. The recruiting team needs to know that they will be able to reach you when they call for the initial phone interview. In your voicemail greeting, your voice should sound clear, confident and professional, with no background noises. Smile when you are recording this greeting—it will make your voice sound even better. For samples of appropriate wording, Google "professional voicemail message."

The email address must also be professional—it must contain your name (or acronyms of it) and nothing else. It is important to align with the standard format of email addresses in the workplace, so it will be easily relatable and memorable. Sample formats you could use are:

    firstnamelastname@gmail.com
    firstname.lastname@yahoo.com
    firstinitiallastname@outlook.com

The executive summary

The executive summary is where your brand statement goes. It's an important aspect of your resumé for one simple reason—it's at the top! We spoke about branding in chapter 2, when you discovered your beliefs, strengths and impact: *why* you do what you do, *how* you put it into practice, and the *impact* it has on the job. It's now time to bring your brand to life. This requires considerable self-reflection and thought as well as a look back into your past and experiences. If you approach it with the right attitude, this activity can be enjoyable for you, as you may uncover details about yourself that you didn't know. Now you might be thinking *Do they expect me to take long walks on the beach and watch the sunset as I dream about my past and reflect upon myself?* Hey, whatever works for you. (For John, it was with a cup of coffee at Starbucks, reinforced by a formal management training program on leadership.)

Creating your brand statement is no easy task. Formal training sessions dedicated just to teaching you this are offered by professional companies. But if you apply the basic information we give you in this book, your brand statement will already stand out from the multitude of resumés with an executive summary (and LinkedIn profile summary) all about being professional and self-motivated and 5 plus years' experience in…

You already have your list of beliefs, strengths and impact from chapter 2. So now it's time to make a brand statement from these elements.

To give you an idea of how to get started, here's an example taken from Connel's brand statement in his own words:

Beliefs

1. Millennials have a lot of potential in our workforce because of their willingness to learn.

2. There is no such thing as perfection. You can always improve.

3. When dealing with customers, always understand the situation from their perspective.

4. If you want to bring about change, it's important to understand why the change is important and to communicate that reason to your team. This way, they will be behind you.

5. The most important aspect of team management is *trust* that your team members are doing their best to perform. They, in turn, must trust that you've got their back.

6. If you want to be noticed, be different.

Strengths

1. Because I think of things from others' perspectives (i.e., my team and customers), I've developed analytical skills that allow me to assess situations fully.

2. Because I am also capable of addressing risks when I see the whole picture, this leads to being a better problem solver than most.

3. Striving to improve and making things better has helped me to become a motivator for others to improve.

4. Because I understand the importance of how more hands can accomplish more work and I acknowledge that others are naturally better than I am at certain tasks, I encourage team effort in everything I do.

5. Because I believe in doing things differently, I think outside the box. When people think of managing a situation in one direction, I find another way that could be better.

Impact

1. My team trusts that I will provide my support with their issues or concerns.

2. I'm the researcher. When given a task, I'll uncover the best way to do it and then customize the solution to fit our needs.

3. People I deal with are aware I get into the details of any problems or concerns being raised.

4. My managers delegate enduring tasks to me because they know I'll persistently see it through to the end.

Connel came up with his beliefs, strengths and impact thinking back into his past, specifically to all those situations that had significant impact on him. These included such events as a major project, a disagreement with a colleague, and a critical decision with two viable options and reflecting on why he had chosen one over the other. Connel also considered what makes him stand out in the team. What is it about him that would lead people to approach him over someone else?

He looked at the above list and came up with the following brand statement:

I enjoy making people's lives easier through technology.

I've been in the IT service management industry for over a decade and if I'm not helping an end user solve a problem, you'll find me talking numbers with the management, or brainstorming a new idea with my team. With me, it's all about change. Bringing about change with calculated risks keeps my job exciting and my team motivated. They know our problems are theirs to solve, and they can rely on my guidance and expertise to coach them through the hurdles. I learn from multiple sources – books, blogs, certification and my managers. I don't like reinventing the wheel. I establish best practices and tweak as required. What do others say about me? They say I'm reliable, approachable, persistent and funny.

He has used the above brand statement in his LinkedIn profile and online resumé. A compact version appears in his one-page hardcopy resumé due to space constraints.

Did you notice that his brand statement is very personal and informal in its approach? When you read most summaries in LinkedIn, you will notice a lot of corporate jargon. Connel's first draft followed that same tone, filled with corporate buzzwords such as collaboration, driven, and of course, passion. This went against one of his most important beliefs—being different—so he quickly realized that he had to rewrite it. Take note that his brand is very people focused, because that's part of his role as team leader.

If you're applying for a technical role, your statement could also talk about your expertise in that field. For example, if you're a database administrator, your belief could be that a company's data is critical to its operations, your strength is data analysis, and your impact is being the person that's able to find data discrepancies. A line in your brand statement could be: "I always seek to automate the management of data and its analysis to preserve its integrity in real time, so that management teams can trust my analysis to make big decisions from big data."

To create your own statement that will appear in your executive summary, use your list of beliefs, strengths and impact. In some instances, you may wish to combine multiple beliefs or strengths into one sentence. Normally, your winning brand statement won't emerge right off the bat. It will take you several reiterations before it feels right.

As you start creating your resumé, you will discover more about yourself and come back to your brand statement and tweak it. Most importantly, seek opinions from people who know you best. It was Connel's wife who made him realize his first draft (yes, filled with corporate jargon) was the most boring thing she'd ever heard in her life!

Remember this: Your brand statement belongs to *you* and it's unique because you alone can create it. We discourage you from having someone else blindly write this brand statement for you. If you're concerned about your writing skills, seek the aid of someone willing to help you out, but *your input* must remain the larger part of the process.

Notice how the brand statement does not contain self-praise? When you look at the opening of a typical resumé, you notice those hard-working, professional, and self-motivated words. Now so overused, these words have lost their meaning in the real world. By contrast, your brand statement is a declaration of what you believe in and what you can do, in the same way any brand is marketed. When Apple markets its latest iPhone, the focus is on the company's beliefs, how the new phone was created and what it can do. Your brand statement, once completed, has to be a reflection of you, and it should also be a promise you can live by. If your brand statement is eye catching enough, the interviewer may ask a question about it. With an *honest* brand statement, you should have no problems answering any questions related to it.

Soft Skills

The soft skills area of your resumé is certainly going to stand out from the rest. Most people just list out their soft skills in bullet form. To make matters even worse, everyone seems to be dipping into the same pool of soft skills and labelling their resumé with the same bland old terms: self learner, highly motivated, and multi-tasking. Yes, these are enviable soft skills to have, but it isn't enough that you just list them out—you must *explain* to the reader how this soft skill applies to you.

Remember our hiring manager from earlier on? She's at it again: "So, you're a multi-tasker? So are the 15 other candidates I'm looking at. Just how are you a multi-tasker exactly? If it means you can text on your phone while in a meeting, that's not the type of multi-tasker I'm looking for."

If, in your resumé, you say, "I'm given responsibilities that cover reporting, scheduling and training, so I'm required to multi-task by managing my time and attention to each focus area," *now* we know what you mean.

So, what soft skills should you write about? First start by making a list of the soft skills from several job descriptions for your target job. If, for example, you're applying for a junior accounting role, head on down to your preferred job search site, and aim to find six to eight job descriptions for this title. They don't have to be current openings—we're not applying for jobs at this stage, but we need what's on the job description. Scan through each of them and make note of the most common soft skills that companies are looking for.

Once you have your list sorted by the most commonly found soft skills, reflect on your experience in the past and write down a single sentence on *how* that soft skills applies to you. If it doesn't apply, skip it and move on to the next one. *Remember, you have to be honest in your resumé.* If you see "Must be able to deal with high levels of stress," and you know from past experience that you crack under pressure, don't speak to it. Move to the next soft skill.

Connel has **bolded** the soft skills in his resumé because these are those infamous keywords that keep appearing in job descriptions for his target job title. It's important to consider keywords because the hiring manager and recruiter have used them in the creation of the job description. Application tracking systems will find your resumé based on those same keywords, so be sure to use them in your resumé. We're not changing that. What we're changing is how those keywords are *explained* in your resumé.

After going through six to eight job descriptions, you may have a pool of 10 to 12 soft skills in your arsenal. Of course, you are not going to use all of them in one resumé, but *save your file*. Remember how we said that every resumé has to be customized to each job you're applying for? Well, when you are applying for any particular position, that job description will have a specified set of required soft skills. This is where you will copy particular soft skills from your pool, selecting the ones that are listed in the job you're applying for, and paste them into your customized resumé. In which order? In the order in which they are listed in that job description. You've just made customizing your resumé a heck of a lot easier this way!

What about your generic resumé, the one that you'll be sending out to the hidden job market? Once again, looking at the six to eight descriptions that you have, find the soft skills that are the most common among all of them and use those for your generic resumé. Select no more than four or five soft skills to avoid spilling over to a second page.

You're still concerned about not having that second page, aren't you? Look at it this way. The reader will also appreciate the fact that you've managed to summarize your experience that relate to the requirements on a single page. You've made his or her job easier while also demonstrating your writing skills—being brief and to the point is a lot harder (and more appreciated) than you think.

Professional experience

The professional experience is where the stories of your past (and present) unfold. To continue following our mantra of being unique and standing out, stay clear of the corporate jargon and avoid stating your responsibilities in a sleep-inducing task-like format. People love stories, and your job experience is a collection of stories. You just have to make sure that you're narrating the *relevant* stories on that one page.

Using the same principles of the soft skills section, the same list of job descriptions can be used. Select the keywords that you spot in there. The keywords may be verbs, processes, other job roles, and anything that stands out in the statement of the responsibility. For the same type of job, variations of the same word might be used from one job description to the next. The below example will give you an idea of what we mean.

This is a typical job description of an HR Administrative Assistant:

1. Providing [**confidential administrative support**] and completing [**research**] on a variety of topics for the Regional Manager/Manager and the respective department.
2. Preparation of [**presentations, reports, correspondence**] and coordination of [**meetings and calendars**].
3. Prepares [**briefing materials**] and documents for meetings.
4. Prepares [**agendas** and **takes minutes at meetings**].
5. Maintains [**document management system**]
6. Handle all recruitment queries in a responsive, [**customer-focused**] way; providing a comprehensive first line of information and advice.
7. Properly handle [**complaints and grievance procedures**]
8. Proficiency with [**MS Office**] applications including Word, Excel, PowerPoint, Outlook.

So now you have your list of keywords that you have bracketed from the job description. List them out if it makes it easier for you to take a snap shot.

Your story begins:

Start by stating the company name and the timeline of service to them. Every story has an introduction, so start with a brief description of the company, *why* you were hired in the first place, and the mission that you had. For an HR Administrative role, the introduction may go like this:

"A major pharmaceuticals company operating in 7 provinces all over the country, with a staff strength of over 5,000 employees. As the company goes through steady expansion and has to deal with a fairly high volume of staff turnover, this keeps the HR department on their toes, with a heavier workload on recruitment, onboarding and offboarding procedures. My job was to work closely with the HR management and their support teams to alleviate the burden of paperwork from their shoulders and ensure a smooth communication flow throughout the team."

This introduction is direct and to the point, giving the reader an idea of the company and environment where you worked. You've positioned yourself as a *problem solver*—paperwork is often a burden to management and something they'd like an administrative person to handle—nice catch!

Now, let's look at the keywords that have been listed. At the top of the job description, you have "confidential administrative support" and "research". It doesn't sound as though these two could be related, and it's rather odd that they are in the same sentence. But hold on, the next keywords are presentation, reports, and correspondence. Perhaps that can be combined with the confidential part. Think back on your experience and how you honoured confidentiality. Yes, you remember now that your manager always told you to maintain confidentiality with paperwork and correspondence. So, your story may go like this:

*"Management was clear on the strict policies of **confidentiality** when I was asked to create reports and **correspondence** of any kind. I prepared **scheduled reports** on employee expenses, monthly reports on salary breakdowns, and monthly reports on vacation and absenteeism. I gathered these reports using combined data from SAP, SharePoint and **Microsoft Office**. I triple checked to make sure that the reports were emailed to the appropriate people before clicking Send. I never received any*

complaints about breaches in confidentiality, and gathered feedback on im-
proving the format and structure of the reports, all of which pleased our
customers*."*

First, note the tone of the story—very conversational, wouldn't you agree? This is how you would describe this responsibility to a friend. Second, you did not compromise any keywords—you used "confidentiality", "Microsoft Office", "reports", "correspondence", and "customer", that were proudly bolded to catch a recruiter's eye. Also note the structure of the story: You began by stating the problems—confidentiality and report creation. Then you described what you did to solve those problems in an easy-to-understand conversational tone, using important keywords. You finished the story by providing the results of your work: no confidentiality breaches and customer satisfaction.

Continue creating the rest of your job responsibilities in the same way. Look to combine keywords using a combination that speaks to *your* experience, so that you can tell a five-to-six-line story using those words. In the example above, you may next want to combine research and presentation because you were required to help management research on various HR initiatives that were industry best practice and create presentations for them.

Storytelling your responsibilities in this conversational tone, while targeting keywords, will create a much more meaningful (and unique) resumé than a point-by-point task-list format. If your past experience can't be wrapped around certain keywords, that's okay. Skip those and use the other keywords. If you're finding that you don't have enough stories to tell based on those keywords, you can talk about other responsibilities that you had. For example, you can start with how you *learned* to do the job. This is especially useful for emerging Millennials who have some work experience. Hiring mangers know that you will have to learn a lot on the job, so writing about the training you did and how you applied that knowledge will be beneficial.

Remember the tip we gave earlier about focusing on the 20 per cent of your job that makes you stand out, as opposed to the 80 per cent of the job that is operational and boring? That can be a challenge because the job description is written to speak to the 80 per cent. It's up to you to *take that boring job description and make it exciting*. Combine keywords into a single story and speak to that part of the responsibility that is 20 per cent. For example, if you are a team leader or manager, and the performance of your team is part of the job description, you may find several lines in the job description talking about coaching, mentoring and conducting performance reviews. 80 per cent of the time, you're giving positive reviews to people, but 20 per cent of the time you have to deal with your high performers and your challenging low performers. Speak to *that* in your story. The hiring manager wants to see how you managed the extremes of your responsibilities. A typical job description for a team leader with relation to team performance is below:

1. Create an engaged workforce by coaching and mentoring team members to develop skills required to provide excellent client experience and proficiency in their role.
2. Guide and motivate the team to meet challenging performance targets.
3. Provide regular, formal and informal feedback and recognition, conduct meetings and create an environment conducive to the exchange of information/ideas.

These three responsibilities can be combined into one story in your resumé:

"*When management set performance targets at the beginning of the year, I decided to schedule two hours every week to monitor my team's targets in the previous week and to provide feedback. For performers who found these targets challenging, I set up bi-weekly, one-on-one* **coaching** *and* **mentoring** *sessions. To motivate the team, I came up with the idea of using our customer satisfaction system to post compliments paid to our team members by the* **client experience***. My top performers came up with new ideas, using additional skills such as scripting and document management, that benefited the team as a whole. As a result of persistent* **feedback** *I provided them, my* **team's performance** *always reached target by the end of the year, and management appreciated my strategy."*

There you go, three requirements from the job description summarized into one 126-word story, using all the keywords from the job description, and focusing on the 20 per cent during which you made unique decisions to manage those responsibilities.

Education and certification

The details of your education and qualifications are safely and proudly in your LinkedIn profile. Job descriptions (at least the ones that we've seen) never contain grade requirements. For the purposes of your resumé, all that a prospective employer wants to know is whether you've acquired the necessary education and certification or not. If the recruiter and hiring manager want more details, they will review your LinkedIn profile or online resumé. Or better yet, they will ask you about it at the interview.

For these two sections, just list out your certifications and highest level of education as shown in the template discussed earlier in this chapter. That's all they need to know when deciding whether or not to give you a call.

Constructing your solution letter (a.k.a. cover letter)

We have intentionally renamed this age-old label because we wanted to focus on what your letter should be about. The standard cover letter stating who or what you are and attempts at splashing your skills and experience in the front has to be done away with. Once again, just like with your resumé, we are going for *impact* and *uniqueness* and most important of all, *personalization.*

Your solution letter is the introduction to your resumé. But unlike your resumé, whose sole purpose is to advance you the interview, the letter's sole purpose is to persuade the readers to open your resumé. Therefore, the objective should be to spark their interest, tickle their curiosity, hit a pain-point nerve in their jobs! Over the years, we have received hundreds of emails from people looking for work. Their cover letter is on the body of the email message. Here are the reasons we would *not* open the resumé:

1. If it's addressed "To whom it may concern" or "Dear Sir or Madam"– ***Delete***
2. If it starts with "I'm looking for a position in…." – ***Delete***
3. If it starts with "I have 5 years' experience in…." – ***Delete***
4. If it explains about what skills and experience the person had in their past job – ***Delete***

These kinds of statements are not unique because *everyone uses them.* Therefore, there is no impact and the letter does not compel the reader to open the resumé. It's not personalized or customized because it says nothing about the reader or the company. Most importantly, it does not address any concerns or problems the reader has at the moment within his or her realm of responsibility.

If you want to construct a letter that holds the attention of the reader and gets that person to open your resumé, it should contain the follow elements:

1. A hook—something thought-provoking, unique and personal that stirs the reader's curiosity
2. A problem—pain point that the hiring manager is currently going through
3. A solution—*you!*
4. A proposal for contact—reaching out

The hook is a set of statements that grabs the reader's attention. What could be more attention grabbing for the reader than a statement about himself or herself? You could write about the reader's accomplishments or some aspect of that position in the company. Or, it could be something about the company and how it relates to the reader. Where can you get this information? Details about the company from Google, news information about the hiring manager from LinkedIn or Google as well. If the company has won an award, you could start with that and congratulate the hiring manager on being part of an award-winning company, with a comment on how his team contributed to the success.

For example:

> *Dear Mr. Ribeiro. I read that Zero2Hired won the Best Workplace for Millennials award for the 6th year in a row. As you are a manager working with the company for 8 years, I want to congratulate you on the leadership skills you bring to your teams that leads to award-winning success.*

You can see how statements like these would be more impactful than "I have 5+ years' experience…" We will discuss telling the reader what you have to offer, but first you have to get that hiring manager interested in what you have to say by complimenting him or her. Once you have the reader hooked, you move on to the meat of your letter—the reader's problem and the solution you bring.

The 'problem' is an educated guess about what the hiring manager is facing at the moment. Think about why your department exists; think about why your manager's job would exist. For example, let's take the accounts receivable department in finance. Their job is essentially to collect money from customers. Some call them credit control. If this department did not exist, no one would ensure that customers are making their payments on time. Without money coming in on time, the business may not function properly—salaries may not be paid, vendors may not be paid, taxes and utilities may not be paid. The company's reputation would be tarnished. We can clearly see the problem that accounts receivable solves.

Now take it a step further—what could the department manager's problem be? He or she would definitely have targets to meet, as set by senior management. The expectation is that a target percentage of payments will be received, and if that percentage is not reached, the department manager will be held accountable. In order to ensure the timely payment of amounts owing, the manager may be cultivating a positive relationship with customers while working closely with sales and handling payment disputes through the sales team. This manager won't have the time to place reminder calls to customers regarding payments that are due, or to work with the invoicing department to determine who the late payers are so that more pressure can be applied. This is the problem that manager is facing.

You must highlight this problem so that it strikes a nerve with the hiring manager. He or she will relate to your message, thinking "this person knows what I'm going through". The above example can be stated in the following manner:

"Accounts receivable plays a crucial role in ensuring a smooth cash flow to the company. As the manager, you must be accountable for strict targets being set by finance management, and while you're busy dealing with customer relations and the sales team, you won't have the time to address the collection process yourself."

Knowing the details of the problem in this way can be challenging, but if you have experience in this field, you should know *something* about any one problem that the department faces. The manager will undoubtedly be juggling other problems, but you don't need to speak to all of them. Pick one, and speak to that. If you're new to the field as an emerging Millennial, *when in doubt, Google it out.* Type in "challenges faced by [*department name*]" and you will see helpful information to get you started.

The solution is where you introduce yourself into the mix and where your solution letter gets its title. You now explain how your skills and expertise solve the problem faced by the hiring manager and the department. Think about the job position and your responsibilities, and connect the dots to your hiring manager. How does your job make his or her life easier? For our ongoing example in accounts receivable, it may be worded something like this:

"With the two years of experience I have gained working in accounts receivable, I can make certain that you will achieve your targets, by handling the day-to-day operations with our customers. Our dues will be collected on time, while you can focus on strategic decisions with the sales team for problematic customers."

Generally, solutions are angled at the hiring manager not having the time to do something because he or she is busy doing something else. That's probably why you were hired in the first place. You may also have special expertise that most accounts receivables folks don't have.

"In the past, I have also used my advanced skills in Excel macros to ensure that the accounts receivable process ran efficiently to meet our targets."

An even better alternative is to speak to a past experience (if you have one) in which you actually *did* solve the manager's problem. This would definitely add more value and impact to your letter. It could flow something like this:

"When I worked for Zero2Hired, 50 per cent of invoices were past their credit due date when I just joined the company. As soon as I understood the policies and culture of the company and its customers, I worked closely with finance and sales to streamline the process, and reduced our aged invoice to 8% in three months."

Fantastic! Now you have a hiring manager who is really curious to know the details of how you did that and wants to give you a call before even *opening* your resumé!

You end the letter with a proposal for contact, which is where you set your goal to actually speak with the person. Personal conversation should always be your goal, as frightening as that may be. It is only through conversation that people are hired, right? Have you ever heard of someone getting a job through text messages alone?

Also, don't put the burden on the other person to contact you. Always demonstrate that you're willing to take action first. All you need is a date and time.

"I hope to have the opportunity to speak with you about the opening you have for an Accounts Receivable Specialist. Please let me know the most suitable time for you, and I'll call you at that time."

The above solution letter is a guideline that you can tweak to suit your specific scenario. If you're applying for a specific advertised role, you will speak to that position in your proposal for contact. Keep length in mind when creating your letters. The key is to keep the solution letter as personalized as possible, short and to the point. In the example above, our letter was just over 200 words—brief enough for the hiring manager to not mind reading it. Now, you will stand out from the swarm of self-centred cover letters that just promote each job seekers' own skills and agenda. Remember, from the reader's perspective, it's not about what you can do. It's about what you can do *for them*.

Takeaways and exercises

You now know how to create a much more impactful conversational resumé that tells stories about your past experience, especially highlighting the 20 per cent of your job that deals with the extremes of your responsibilities. No boring mundane stuff. And you are doing this without sacrificing those all-important keywords that recruiters and application tracking systems are looking for.

You also have a new methodology for creating a solution letter, one that is the *definition* of personalization. It will hook your reader and prompt that hiring manager to open your resumé. Keep it personal. Keep it short. Keep it about the reader and not about you. Remember, you are a solution to their problem, and not the other way around.

We've also discussed the differences between the hiring manager and the recruiter. As we will see in chapter 6, it's essential to be in direct contact with these folks. Your conversational resumé and solution letter won't work with a recruiter who is in assembly line mode. For this reason, you want to find back entrances to getting your resumé noticed.

Exercise:

Your exercise for this chapter is to create your first conversational resumé. It won't be customized to an advertised job just yet. For now, you will create a generic version that will be used to tackle the *hidden job market*, using the compilation of six to eight job descriptions that you collected earlier on, and writing stories to address the most common responsibilities in them.

We can't create a solution letter just yet, because there is no such thing as a generic solution letter. We will tackle that in chapter 6.

We now move on to other areas you need to be prepared for, before you start contacting recruiters and hiring managers and applying for jobs.

CHAPTER 5

MAKING YOURSELF JOB READY

You are not done preparing yet! We know, we know. You've spent all this time getting your resumé done and you're eager to get it out there. A little more patience and effort is all we're asking for. We don't want you to blow *any* chance of getting that interview.

This chapter is about the other areas outside of your resumé for which you need to be prepared. Did you realize that an interview can occur at any moment after you submit your resumé? This means that you *must* be fully prepared for an interview from the moment you submit your first resumé, otherwise you risk missing out on your opportunity. Remember, the interview doesn't begin at an office behind a desk. It begins the moment you answer that phone call from the recruiter or hiring manager— and that phone could be ringing without any warning.

The obvious

It's time to go shopping for a new outfit! We're not experts on this matter, so we won't be giving any fashion advice here. We don't know the difference between a pashmina and a tie. Our motto is *"When in doubt, Google it out."* Hop onto the search engine, search for "interview outfits" and make your choices. This advice is for men and women—*if you don't own a blazer, now's the time to get one.* We'll have more to say about the importance of appearance later, but for now, just know that we have both denied applicants a job because of their choice of attire at the interview. No matter which company you are interviewing for, being formally dressed at an interview is a *standard practice* across the globe. It doesn't matter if your inside intel in the company has confirmed that everyone walks around in flip-flops. Until you get the job, your appearance and demeanor must remain formal and professional.

Next, you'll be needing a cell phone that is reachable at any time, with voice mail enabled. Connel once received a call for an interview while on another interview! You never know when the employer comes knocking on your wireless door. Don't let *any* opportunity pass you by.

While on the subject of communication, you need a *professional* email address. We covered this briefly when we designed your resumé. If your current email address does not have your name, you need to set up a new one. The email address must be professional by containing your name, just like you would have in a corporate environment. If it's unavailable, try variations with numbers. We discourage using underscores ("_"), as they are not easily visible in hyperlinks. You can try the following variations:

Firstnamelastname (e.g., johnribeiro@gmail.com)
Firstname.lastname (e.g., connel.valentine@yahoo.com)
Firstname-lastname (e.g., john-ribeiro@outlook.com)
Firstnamelastname## (e.g., connelvalentine81@aol.com)

Get qualified

During the process of creating your resumé in the previous chapter, you looked at six to eight job descriptions from your target job title. While looking at those job descriptions, apart from the job experience and soft skills, you would have also seen qualifications required for the job. If it's a project management role, you may have seen the requirement of a diploma in project administration, or even a PMP certification for more senior roles. If it's a junior accountant role, you may have seen requirements for ACA or CIMA. Take the hint! Although we said in chapter 1 that a lack of certain qualifications *may* be overlooked by the employer, if you're seeing it often enough in job descriptions, chances are that it's a minimal requirement.

For entry-level roles, you may not have this problem. If, however, you are an established Millennial with a few years of experience under your belt or wanting to switch industries, you need to be aware of this. If you have the time and the money to pursue a certification, go for it!

> Connel once applied for an IT Service Desk team lead position at a logistics company. The recruiter called him after a few days to say that the position was unionized and that the union rules required the person in that job to have a Comptia A+ certification. Connel asked her how long the position would remain open and was told at least for another two weeks. A week and half later, he called the recruiter back to announce that he had obtained his certification and to ask, "What's next?" Connel was fortunate that the Comptia A+ course is affordable and obtainable online, with a requirement to write the exam at an authorized exam centre.

So if you see a common trend in professional qualifications for the job you're trying to get, do your best to seek out that qualification or certification as quickly as possible. But at the same time, don't let it stop you from applying for the job. You never know which employer may overlook that 'need', especially if you have a winning personality for which they would be willing to compromise a qualification.

Get tech-ready

So now that your generic resumé (from chapter 4) is primed and you are confident about the integrity of its contents, it's time to plug it into the World Wide Web! Upload your resumé and professional profile to all your favourite job search sites. LinkedIn deserves special attention, and we'll cover that next.

From chapter 3, you should now have a strong sense of specific companies that you'd want to work for. Visit the websites of the medium to large organizations on your list and upload your generic resumé to their career site. If you're targeting smaller start-ups, you may not see this option on their websites.

You will need a printer for hardcopies of your resumé. You can always use your public library's printer, but ink jet printers that can quickly and easily print black-and-white documents are quite affordable these days.

Now is the time to think about the manner in which you will organize your job search information. As we will explain in the next chapter, every action in your job search process needs to be logged. You could get a call from an employer following a job application that you made weeks ago. Doesn't it make sense to keep and properly organize all the information you gathered for that application so you can refer back to the forgotten details? Choose the method of document management that you're the most comfortable using. Your method can be as easy and effective as organizing the details of each job into its own folder on your Windows desktop. (It can also be a physical folder with hardcopies of the information you collect.) Connel's personal choice is to use Microsoft OneNote, a fantastic (but not free) piece of software that allows the user to keep information organized.

Your LinkedIn profile

Apart from all the social networking tools that you undoubtedly use on a daily basis, when you're on the hunt for work, LinkedIn should be your go-to social networking site.

In June 2016, Microsoft announced that it would be buying LinkedIn for $26.2B, a strategy that had many of us wondering what was in store for LinkedIn in the future. Without a doubt, Microsoft has a dominant presence in the corporate world, and today it's rare to find an office environment that is not using a Microsoft product. This leads us to believe that LinkedIn is going to be even more of a corporate standard for human resource departments to source its candidates, as Microsoft may start devising ways of integrating its already popular office tools with LinkedIn. It's what they did when they bought Skype, and created Skype for Business!

It's important to understand why businesses use LinkedIn to find candidates. When a role becomes available in a company, the hiring process can become tedious and expensive. The HR folks need time to find the 'perfect candidate', and there are always hundreds, if not thousands of people who are willing to fill that role. The recruiters need a mechanism to filter out candidates who would definitely not qualify for the role, allowing them to focus their precious time on only dealing with candidates who actually have a shot at the job.

Even today, companies use hiring agencies for this filtering process. It's smart and efficient, but expensive. The hiring agencies have various strategies for making a profit from the filtering service they provide. This is where LinkedIn comes in. From a recruiting perspective, it's essentially an online filtering process. For a reasonable fee, company recruiters use LinkedIn to filter candidates by qualification, location, and whatever other criteria are deemed necessary. This process is cheap and fast, and employers can rely on their own trusted expertise to find the right candidates. We have personally hired excellent candidates from LinkedIn, and Connel has even been contacted for phone interviews through LinkedIn. We are not saying that LinkedIn is better or worse than using agencies, as each has its own advantages. It's just important for you to know that LinkedIn is also a popular candidate sourcing tool. A recruiter survey conducted by JobVite in 2016 revealed that 87 per cent of recruiters find LinkedIn the most effective social media network when vetting candidates in the job hiring process.

So, if you are looking for work, and have not set up a LinkedIn profile, you're not getting as much professional visibility in the job market as you need. Fire up your computer and visit LinkedIn ASAP!

Once your account is created, the first order of business is to set up your profile. The good news is that with your *generic* conversational resumé written, most of the detail has already been created for your LinkedIn profile. It's just a matter of copying and pasting the parts of your resumé into the relevant sections of your new profile. Furthermore, while you're limited to two pages on your resumé, LinkedIn is the forum where you can expand the content of your knowledge and experience without worrying about space constraints.

Once again, Google is your best bet in gathering the useful tips on completing your LinkedIn profile. Google "tips on creating LinkedIn profile," and you'll come across a full string of recommendations.

Here are a couple of basic tips that will help you get started:

Your professional photograph is essential. No LinkedIn profile should exist without a picture. According to a spokesperson from LinkedIn, having a profile picture increases your chances of being viewed by 14 times. Now please don't whip out your smartphone and take a selfie or upload the first thing you find in your photo library.

LinkedIn is where you portray the *professional* you. Wear what you bought for the interview, ideally a suit or blazer, visit a studio and have a quick professional photo taken. Or if you know someone who's a shutterbug, ask that person if he or she is willing to do it for you. The best place to get an idea of what to look for is **Pinterest**, where you can search "professional headshots" for a range of fantastic ideas to show your photographer of choice what you're looking for. To this day, we're shocked at the low-quality photographs we see on LinkedIn. It really doesn't send a professional message to the potential employer scouting your profile.

Your professional headline appears just under your name. It should reflect the target job title on your resumé.

Location and industry are extremely important, as employers will filter their searches based on these criteria.

Summary is the first content an employer sees in your profile. It is the brand statement you have creatively worded. You may choose to have a summarized version in your resumé, but your LinkedIn profile will have it in full. Remember, there are fewer space constraints with LinkedIn.

Experience can be copied over from the professional experience section of your resumé. Here is where you can take liberties in expanding your experience as much as you'd like. Employers will just scroll over the sections that don't interest them.

Certifications is where all your formal training should be displayed. The CCNAs, PMPs, ITILs, CIMAs, etc. go here—essentially, any certified education that you pursued outside of school, college or university. School-related achievements belong in the Education section.

Projects should be taken from the projects section of your resumé if you have one. Once again, you can make use of the space offered in your LinkedIn profile. Add the details of *all* projects that you have accomplished and played a critical role in. If you're an emerging Millennial, be sure to include projects that you did in school.

Volunteer section is where you will list in your volunteer work, and you should elaborate the details of this work. Large enterprises usually have a charity wing in their organization and invite employees to volunteer and contribute to the company's (and department's) community fundraising and awareness efforts. Business owners like to give back to the community and use their business as leverage to do that. Showing that you are willing to do volunteer work is a bonus.

The above points should be enough to get your profile started. As you can see, most of the work has already been done in your resumé. And those details that you were aching to explain but didn't have room for in your resumé can be added here.

Prepare answers to interview questions

You might be wondering why we are discussing answering interview questions so early in the game, when you haven't even applied for jobs yet. You may be thinking that once you get the interview, you can wing it or adlib your way through because you're confident in your abilities to answer any question that is thrown your way. This is a fatal mistake that one of your authors made in the past!

You must prepare in advance the answers for questions that you could be asked by the interviewer. Otherwise, you will leave the interview thinking *Oh, why did I say that? I should have said the other thing!* Trust us when we say from experience that it's *not* a warm and fuzzy feeling. In reality, that one question may have made the difference between landing the job or not.

It's impossible to know in advance every question that will be asked at an interview, but there are some standard questions. Of course, the deciding-factor make-or-break questions will depend on the type of job itself and on the skill of the interviewer. Our goal in this book is not to address every single question that could be asked. Together, however, we will create a pool of knowledge that is based on your past experience. This pool will be well thought out, and revised and revisited as you see fit. You will find yourself picking topics from this pool of knowledge to answer the interview questions that you are asked. To create this knowledge, we have organized the questions into sections. Each section is differentiated by an area of your skill or experience, for example strengths, weaknesses, relationships, etc.

Your introduction

The *first* question that you will inevitably be asked will be extremely general. It may sound like this: "Tell me about yourself" or this: "Tell me about your past experiences" or this: "What has your career been like so far?" (There *is* a wrong answer to this question by the way, and that is to start talking about your personal life: "Well, I was born in Vancouver, and then moved to…")

The interviewer wants to know *what you have done in the past that can relate to the job at hand.* He or she want to know what you can do for the department. The interviewer is also observing how you answer an unstructured open-ended question. The topic you choose for this answer demonstrates where your focus lies. Your list of strengths from chapter 2 will play an important role in this answer, as you should provide them as part of your introduction. After all, your strengths are an important part of your brand. You can tailor your answer by speaking to different strengths, based on the job you're applying for. More on that in chapter 8, when you're prepping for the interview.

The following areas can be covered for this answer. Bear in mind that your answer should be tailored in a way that speaks to the organization's needs. The question may be "Tell me about yourself," but the interviewer is *really* asking "Tell me about what you have to offer me."

1. **Years of experience:** You have x years of experience to offer to this position.

2. **Industries you have worked for:** In those x years you offer experience in this specific industry or industries.

3. **Beliefs and strengths:** You will offer one or two strengths and beliefs from your list in chapter 2. Use your brand statement from your resumé if you need to. For the purposes of your introduction, you are telling the interviewer, "These are the main strengths I developed to offer to your team."

4. **A story that supports your strength:** You can now give an example of a success story that references these strengths. Think about a major achievement or accomplishment, your involvement in it, how your strength applied to this scenario, and what was achieved from it.

The tell-me-about-yourself question is important and must be well rehearsed. That's why we have given it special attention. It is a first impression question—the interviewer is analyzing your communication skills, getting a feel for your personality, and keeping an ear open for the focus of your story. It is therefore important that this question is answered with both confidence and enthusiasm. If you're fresh out of school, any project work that you've done would count as professional experience here, as would volunteer work. You can also cover why you've chosen this field to start off your career. We recommend writing your introduction down and rehearsing it. Try not to memorize it word for word, because it is going to sound robotic and that's off-putting to the listener.

Here is an example of a tell-me-about-yourself answer for a person applying for an IT Infrastructure engineer role:

"I started in IT service management about 8 years ago working for the medical and travel security services industry. During that time, I worked closely with end users, from junior employees up to C-level executives, supporting their IT needs and requirements. My technical abilities were also recognized by my manager who entrusted me to administer back end infrastructure systems as well. From this experience, I gained knowledge and strengths in customer service and the management of critical IT systems. In that role, the technology I managed was relied on heavily by the critical assistance centre that operated 24/7. I created a disaster recovery site with a fully-mirrored setup of our primary location, complete with a backup server room and office facilities to host 20 staff members. During outages, even at 2 a.m., I would hustle to the office and initiate business continuity plans and organize the failover of IT services and employees to the disaster recovery site. Simultaneously, I would engage our on-call support vendors to fix the issue, all the while keeping management informed on the progress and updates via text messages. This experience taught me the critical nature of IT service and the skills to keep calm under pressure, while ensuring that the business's customer experience was not harmed during an IT-related outage.

> Note: the C-level are the highest-ranking executives in senior management, with titles beginning with 'C' (for 'chief'), such as chief executive officer (CEO), chief operations officer (COO), and chief financial officer (CFO).

This introduction was tailored to strengths and a story for a role where the job was for an IT infrastructure engineer. Notice the emphasis on "critical" service—this is the problem that an IT infrastructure engineer is expected to solve for his manager—to make sure that the sometimes-unpredictable IT infrastructure does not fail. And when it does, the fix is made with the knowledge of its extreme urgency. Likewise, you will need to prepare an introduction that will speak to strengths and stories in your area of expertise. With a well-prepared introduction completed, you must now prepare a list for the knowledge areas below.

The next exercise follows a simple process. You will first be required to list out the various knowledge areas that are discussed in the next section. Then think about a story or scenario that supports each knowledge area. We've given you examples for each knowledge area to get you started, but as always, this is *your career* and *your life*! We encourage you to always tweak or add more, as you see fit.

Our reason for using this approach is the fact that recruiters encourage their hiring managers to follow a situational or behavioural interview methodology, commonly referred to as S.T.A.R.—Situation, Task, Action, Result. This methodology has variations, but the basic concept is simple—take the interviewee back to a time-and-place scenario or **S**ituation, ask questions related to the **T**ask that person was given, the **A**ctions he or she took, and what was the **R**esult or impact of there actions. This is why it's important to think of *scenarios* and *stories* in your pool of knowledge as answers to interview questions. The interviewer will expect this. (Refer our appendix for more details on the STAR method.)

A word of caution—as you select your stories and scenarios, be mindful of being *brief* and *to the point*. Interviewees who provide long-winded monologues lose their audience's interest, and this is another reason why preparation is so important. Also, be careful when you support a story with the word 'we'. The employer wants to know what *you* did in that situation. If you're taking credit for someone else's work, you will eventually be found out and that will set you back.

Knowledge area 1: Your strengths

Exercise:

What do you do differently from others? You thought of examples when you created your brand statement. Now list them out in bullet point form and think of a STAR story that supports each strength. Think about the times when your boss or professor complimented you for what you accomplished.

An example is below.

> ***Documentation Skills:*** *(**S**) When my company was going through an ISO audit, (**T**) I was required to document every aspect of our operations. (**A**) I created those documents and stored them on SharePoint, making sure to follow corporate policy guidelines and templates. (**R**) Management expressed appreciation of my efforts, especially since we passed the audit with flying colours.*

> ***Working under pressure:*** *(**S**) During month-end reporting deadlines, some members of the finance department always panic and get riled up about working late hours. (**T**) Realizing that stress kills productivity, I aimed to keep the mood as light hearted as possible. (**A**) Through the month-end stage, I offered my help, used cheerful humour, and made sure that the team was nourished with food and drinks. (**R**) We managed to hit our deadlines consistently every month, and our team members consistently received an annual performance bonus every year.*

The above examples are very brief, but give you an idea of how the STAR technique is applied. Likewise, come up with as many strengths as you can confidently support with stories and scenarios, and elaborate on them. If you cannot support your strength with a story, it's very likely you don't possess it!

The types of questions that may use this knowledge area include:

1. What are you good at?

2. What are you well known for?

3. Why does your manager need you?

4. What can you contribute to this department that others cannot?

Knowledge area 2: Your weaknesses

Stay away from clichés such as being a perfectionist and workaholic. The hiring manager is looking for is a *real* weakness that you've identified with yourself and how you are planning to resolve it.

Exercise:

Think about what aspects of your previous job you did *not* like doing, but had to. That could be a source of weakness. If you're fresh out of college, a lack of experience is your easiest choice on a weakness.

List your weaknesses in bullet point form, and explain how you are addressing them.

Here are some examples:

> ***Lack of experience***: *I don't have experience in marketing, but I'm taking a course on the subject that will complete in two months. I also frequently read blogs and articles on the subject. I am currently being mentored by a marketing expert to get more information about the field.*

> ***I hate mundane tasks***: *I prefer change over repetitiveness, but I realise that repetitive work is a vital part of the job. To manage it, I try and finish it as early as possible in the day, when my mind is fresh to handle that work without compromising on its quality.*

Highlighting your weaknesses honestly in this way will not cost you the job. Saying that you *don't* have a weakness is a sign of *dishonesty* and *self-righteousness* and a big detracting factor. Questions you may be asked are:

1. What are your weaknesses?
2. What are you currently improving about yourself?
3. Why should I hire you if you don't have experience in this field?

Knowledge area 3: Your accomplishments

Exercise:

Think back to your major projects on the job, or if you're a fresh grad, the projects you did in school.

What was the project about? Who was involved? What was at stake? What was the result? What was *your* part in the project?

Accomplishments need not be limited to projects. It could also be about something you newly learned *and* implemented in your work life.

Here are some examples:

__HR Software Implementation:__ Our HR management and IT department were working on the implementation of a software program to automate salary slips. I worked closely with the IT team of three developers and acted as a liaison between HR operations and the IT team to communicate and formalize the payroll process. The software cost $80,000, and the team was on a tight deadline to begin automated payroll by the start of the next year. By working three months with late nights and six-day weeks, we successfully implemented it on time.

Be sure to select projects in which you were *actively involved*. If you're trying to take credit for someone else's work, the interviewer can call your bluff and it's game over. Typical questions:

1. What are your biggest accomplishments?
2. Tell me about a major project you worked on.

Knowledge area 4: Job-specific situations when things went right

Every job has some form of daily operational work that takes up 80 per cent of your time. The hiring manager will kick in with the STAR methodology here, starting with "Tell me about a time when…" This manager wants to know about how your day typically progresses and various scenarios that you have encountered while handling the daily operational tasks. These questions are specific to the role that you're applying for, so they will vary, depending on the job title.

Exercise:

Look into the common responsibilities of the job title, and think about an exceptional story that stands out for each.

For example:

> ***Handling irate customers:*** *I recall an occasion when a customer was upset because she had been waiting a while for an item to be delivered. Since we were the customer service team, we received her call. The customer wanted to speak to the supervisor, but I assured her that I would personally look into the matter for her. I reviewed the details of her case, empathized with her and made her feel that I understood her pain completely. This calmed her down. I was then able to convince her to wait another two days for logistics to contact her, as per their standard response time.*

You should spend substantial time on this knowledge area, because it's closely related to your operations—the meat and potatoes of your job. Think about all the common aspects of your job and a positive, standout story for each.

Knowledge area 5: Job-specific situations when things went wrong

Hiring managers are fully aware that work is not always rainbows and sunshine. They expect things to go wrong and, just like for their questions about your weaknesses, they expect *honest* answers. They want to know first what went wrong, then what you learned from it, and finally, how you can prevent the negative outcome from happening again in the future.

Exercise:

If possible, use the same operational list you created above, and add a story with a not-so-happy-ending to each point. This way, you'll have an example of when *things went right* for that situation, and an example of when *things went wrong*.

If we were to follow the same example above, it might sound like this:

Handling irate customers: *There was a time when an irate customer started abusing me over the phone. I reacted emotionally. I didn't abuse him back, but my tone became sarcastic, which aggravated the situation even more. This customer eventually demanded to speak to my supervisor who handled the situation. Although my supervisor backed me up, sensing that the customer was way out of line, I should have managed my emotions better. Now I always keep my guard up at the start of every call. If I sense an aggravated tone, I remain calm and professional, and mentally focus on the solution to the problem.*

There are some interviewers who may dwell on when things go wrong. These types of questions can get tricky, so it's important to prepare for them:

1. When did you make a mistake?
2. Tell me about a tough situation you faced?
3. How do you handle a tough customer?

Knowledge area 6: Interactions with your team

For this knowledge area, think about your relationships with your manager and your teammates.

Exercise:

Think about any stories or situations that involved either of them. Think about occasions when your manager asked you to do something that you agreed to and other times when you didn't agree. How did you handle it? Think about efforts you accomplished as a team. Think about disagreements you had with individual team members and what you did to resolve the situation. Think about an occasion when you coached or mentored somebody else.

Some questions that may come up to form these stories include:

1. How would your manager describe you (in three words)?
2. How would your team members describe you (in three words)?
3. Tell me about a time when your manager asked you to do something that you didn't agree with?
4. Tell me about a time you accomplished something big with team effort?
5. How do you manage employees who are not performing?

Knowledge area 7: Your career—past, present and future

Your career is an important part of your life and is intimately tied to the job you are about to be hired for. The hiring manager wants to make sure that you will be happy there and stick around. Your past will reveal how you've progressed, and he or she will want to know whether the job at hand is something you want to do, and whether you hold a future with this new organization.

Exercise:

Think about your past experience and what you like about the job and the industry that you are (or were) in. Consider where you want to go and the steps you are taking to pursue your goals.

Some of the questions you may be asked are:

1. Why do you want to work in this field?
2. What do you like about this industry?
3. Why did you change jobs so often?
4. Where do you see yourself in five years?

These examples give an idea of what you need to prepare for. Of course, there are many more example questions available online. Collect as many stories as you can for each, and add more knowledge areas if you like. This pool of knowledge is a valuable resource that can prepare you for those tough interview questions.

Technical interview questions

Depending on your field, you may also be asked technical interview questions. Being in the IT industry, as job applicants we have been asked these in almost every interview. This is a good time to review the requirements of the job description and use it to figure out what types of technical questions may come your way.

Exercise:

Once again, *when in doubt, Google it out.* Search for "technical interview questions for…" where you include your target job title.

Also, from the six to eight job descriptions you reviewed for your resumé, look for any technical gaps between your skills and expertise and what is being asked in the job description.

As stated before, as long as you can do 70 per cent of the requirements, the employer will seriously consider you for the job. But that doesn't mean you won't be asked about the 30 per cent of the job description that you can't do. Be prepared to answer any questions that could arise from that.

References

These days, many hiring managers ask for references. They know all too well the steep costs of hiring the wrong person for the job, so they want to make sure they're making the right decision by asking your previous employers for their opinion of you. We often receive referral calls for contractors on our team who are nearing the end of their contract term and are applying for jobs elsewhere.

Be extremely careful with the people you select for your references. You have to be on good terms with them, and keep in constant contact with them through social networking. The last thing you'd want is for a hiring manager to be 99 per cent sold on hiring you—until the call is made to your reference who turns your image around with a negative review.

Your references could be your old managers, colleagues who worked on the same team as you, or even your university or college professors. They will be contacted to provide their opinions on the quality of your work along with the all-important character reference. Be certain these folks have only positive and supportive things to say about you. You must extend the courtesy of asking them *permission* to be used as a reference. You wouldn't want them to be caught unaware with a random phone call or email from an employer. This could annoy them and lessen their opinion of you.

Obviously if you're currently a full-time employee, you wouldn't use your current manager as a reference. The interviewer should completely understand. If, however, you're currently working under a contract that is nearing the end, your current employer should also be willing to be used as a reference, especially if there is no intention of extending your current contract. Managers know that people nearing the end of their contract are actively looking for work elsewhere.

Takeaways and exercises

In this chapter, we covered the remainder of what you need to be prepared for the job search. Wardrobe is important, so make sure you've found a professional outfit for the interview.

We also covered any qualification gaps that you may need to close if you've seen those qualifications recurring over the six to eight job descriptions you've reviewed.

We talked about how to become 'tech ready' with easy access to a printer and an update to your LinkedIn profile.

The key takeaway from this chapter is preparation for the interview through creating a pool of knowledge and stories to answer questions. Follow the widely-used STAR methodology. Be sure to prepare yourself for the technical questions as well. Take your time and focus on creating the stories that form your knowledge base and revisit, rehearse and update them as you see fit.

Finally, we covered the importance of keeping in touch with your references and asking their permission to be used as a reference.

An exercise is associated with each section of this chapter. Make sure you complete everything from shopping for your interview outfit to speaking to your references.

Your chapter 5 checklist:

1. Interview outfit
2. Cell phone and voicemail
3. Professional email address
4. Qualifications (as required)
5. Generic resumé—upload to job search sites and to career sites of companies on your list
6. Reliable printer
7. Documentation process
8. LinkedIn profile
9. Professional photo
10. STAR answers for interview questions:
    a. Strengths
    b. Weaknesses
    c. Accomplishments
    d. Things went right
    e. Things went wrong
    f. Team interactions
    g. Career goals
11. Job-related technical questions
12. References

Now you are fully prepared to start your job hunt. While you should hustle to get your prep work completed as soon as possible, look at the calendar as well. The start of the new year is the optimal time when companies may have a fresh new budget to start hiring. So, if you're approaching the end of the year, work to complete the prep work so you can quickly start applying for jobs during the spike in job opportunities available from January onwards.

With your generic resumé polished, your LinkedIn profile glowing with the details of your achievements, your target job title locked in your sights, and your answers prepared for any questions thrown your way, you are ready. It's time to shift into high gear and prepare to embrace those interview calls.

CHAPTER 6

THE JOB TRACK PROCESS

Here's how Connel got his job at the organization he started to work for in 2015. He had arrived in Canada with no experience working in North America, but with about 10 years of international experience in IT Services under his belt. He was passionate about the field of IT and he knew that's where he wanted to be, so his target job titles were IT Analyst, IT Engineer, and IT Specialist.

Connel had already completed all of the prep work in the previous chapters by the time he started job hunting. Then he saw the position of IT Service Desk Analyst advertised on LinkedIn. The hiring recruiter's name was posted right next to the opening. Connel customized both his solution letter and resumé and applied for the job on LinkedIn as required. After finding the recruiter's email address, Connel emailed her directly, attaching both his solution letter and conversational resumé. Initially, he received an Out of Office reply. The manager was on vacation and would be back in two days.

Two days later, this intrepid job hunter sent a follow-up email. This time he received a reply: "Thanks for reaching out. It turns out there was a mistake in this posting and I'm not actually responsible for this position, but I'm cc'ing this message to the recruiter for this new opening." Aha! A golden contact! He thanked the first recruiter for her reply and began an email conversation with the appropriate recruiter who, much to Connel's relief, responded. The next day (ironically while Connel was waiting at a coffee shop before a scheduled interview with *another* company), the recruiter called him, and a phone interview began. It went very well, leaving Connel with mixed feelings of confidence and hope that there would be a call back the next day. The recruiter did call… and with an update.

Apparently, the posted job that Connel had been applying for was already filled. Of course, he was disappointed, and especially because it was a fantastic company to work for. The next words from the recruiter went like this: "However, we do have another opening available. It's a Service Desk Team Leader position. In fact, the position that you originally applied for directly reports to this new team leader position. Looking at your resumé, management thought you were more qualified for this job." Of course, this new position paid way more money than the original job he'd applied for. Connel was on cloud nine!

The interview was arranged, and that's where he met his future co-author John Ribeiro. It must have gone well because he landed the job! Total time spent from the day he started looking for work to the day he accepted the offer letter? Two weeks!

A year later, Connel was attending internal training when he bumped into the recruiter who had arranged for that hiring interview. Connel just had to ask, with all the candidates who applied for the job, why did *he* get a call? The recruiter said the only reason he called was because he was cc'd in that email from the first recruiter (whose name was mistakenly put up on LinkedIn)—that had caught his attention. This recruiter also admitted that if he had seen Connel's resumé through the application tracking system, he probably would have ignored it.

With that illuminating story, let the hunt begin! What you're about to experience in this chapter is a tried and tested process that was followed when Connel was on the lookout for work. Assuming you have committed to the prep work form the previous chapters, you're going to transform your passive job hunt process into an active one.

If there ever was an instruction guide on finding a job, this is it! Maybe you aren't the instruction guide type, but we're assuming that you've picked up this book because going with your gut hasn't worked out for you so far. Now's the time to start *getting it right the first time*—from here on end.

Every day you're not working, you're missing out on job opportunities, development and money in the bank. So, let's get hustling!

The job track

A quick description: The job track is a sequential series of steps that any particular job application will follow—from the online application right through to the interview. You will be juggling multiple job tracks simultaneously because you will be applying for more than one job at a time. This is why having that organization folder is essential for tracking purposes, as mentioned in chapter 5. Each job track can last for up to two weeks and will end in one of two ways: you either get the job, or you don't. So, let's take a look at how you run through the job track for an advertised job.

Day 1

Step 1: Target a job

Scout for jobs online using the job sites that you're already familiar with and lock in on a job that you're confident you can do. Remember, you don't have to meet 100 per cent of the requirements—as long as you can nail 60 to 70 per cent of them, you're solid. Be sure to also check for and review career or job sections on the websites of the companies that you're targeting.

When you've found a job that you can do, copy and paste the job description and the company into your online organization folder for your records. This is the folder where you keep all information relevant to this job track, so name it appropriately (e.g., job position, job code or ID, and company). This can either be as simple as a physical file (for which you'll need to print hard copies of everything), or a digital folder, or a tab in Microsoft OneNote.

Step 2: Customize your conversational resumé

Of course, it would be tempting to use the generic conversational resumé you created in chapter 4, but if you really want the job, you must make the added effort of customizing your resumé. You don't have to redo your resumé from scratch. Follow the same process of noting down the *keywords* from the job description, as you did when you created your resumé from chapter 4.

You should find several similar keywords to those you found before creating your generic resumé, so the stories about your professional experience that you created there will still apply here. You are looking for *new keywords* that were not included in your generic resumé. In this case, you want to replace some of what's there with new or tweaked stories for the professional experience section of this customized resumé. Tailoring your resumé to this one advertised job description involves the same process you followed from the six to eight job descriptions you used from chapter 4.

Also, you need to reorder the stories on your resumé so that they synchronize with the order of the keywords on the job description. Remember our grocery list theory? The keywords and responsibilities at the top of the job description are *most important to the hiring manager*, so you want to hit him or her with those stories first.

Don't forget the soft skills. Same principle and process. Capture the keywords from the soft skills being asked for in the job description and speak to those as well, ordered in the same sequence as in the job description.

You may find this process takes time initially, but after a couple of job applications, you'll find that you have a story to tell for most of the keywords being asked. You can just refer back to the same job experience, copying and pasting these stories from previous customized resumés for newly-tailored resumés.

Step 3: Finding the key players

You're going to find at least two (if not three) contacts that you will deal with directly for this job. We wouldn't be surprised if that scares you— once upon a time, it absolutely terrified us! Like it or not, this is how the game is played—beat the competition by standing out and working around (or ahead of) the application tracking system. If you want to shorten the painful time spent looking for a job, you must make direct contact with the people who can hire you

The hiring manager is your prime target. This is the person who created the vacancy and who has the authority and final say on who is hired for the job. This is also the person who has a problem that your potential new job will solve.

The recruiter (a.k.a. Talent Acquisition) is the person with the job of finding candidates to fill an advertised vacancy. Recruiters usually work under HR management and are utilized by hiring managers to employ their online application system to amass the hordes of resumés from internal and public applicants.

A Senior manager from the department hiring you is also a key player from the perspective of influence. Most likely, this person will be your hiring manager's boss or a level higher and the person who authorized the budget for your position. Capturing this individual's attention and recommendation will be helpful.

You might be wondering why it's important to solicit the contact of a member of the senior management (VIP) of the department to which you're applying. There is an irony to VIPs when it comes to the job track process. VIPs could be directors, vice-presidents and even C-level executives (CIO, CFO etc.). For junior to mid-level jobs (targeted by most Millennials), VIPs are the least interested in dealing with you. Yet they are the ones who can potentially provide the most *leverage* to your application. While they will not be directly responsible for hiring for positions three to four levels below them, they are definitely aware of the managers (who report to them) who have that responsibility. And the VIPs *delegate* operational work (such as the hiring process) to these managers under them. Just imagine if you captured the attention of a VIP with your impressive conversational resumé and solution letter, and that VIP forwarded it to the hiring manager reporting to him or her, with a delegated note with the direction "Look into this." Your resumé would now have the undivided attention of the hiring manager because it came from the boss. How's that for a twist in your favour? Keep this in mind for later.

Step 4: Find contact information

Now that you know the types of people to contact, the question is *where do you find them?* LinkedIn! By far the easiest resource, LinkedIn allows you to find people using the Advanced Search and filtering them by the company name (which you already know), the department and even job title. Also, if the job is advertised on LinkedIn, chances are you'll see the name of the recruiter responsible for that job posting. However, LinkedIn may give you a name and title, but it may not necessarily give you contact details—most people are private about that.

So now you have the name, you'll need an email address. Let's say your contact's name is John Ribeiro.

First, you can try just Googling the company name and "email address". So, if you're applying for a job at Zero2Hired, use Google to search "Zero2Hired email address". Look through the websites that come up in the search results. With any luck, you'll get at least one person's email address. You don't care about that person's email address, what you care about is the *format* of the email address. Usually, the most common formats are:

Firstname.lastname (john.ribeiro@zero2hired.com)
Firstnamelastname (johnribeiro@ zero2hired.org)
Firstinitiallastname (jribeiro@ zero2hired.ca)

With the person's name, and the format of the email address, just swap it out and you have the email address of your target contact. However, it's not always so straightforward. If this process does not yield an example email from the company, you can also review the company's website to find an email address there. You can normally find an address in the Contact Us section or the Careers section. Most likely, you will find something like info@zero2hired.com or careers@zero2hired.ca.

What you have now is the *domain name* of this organization's email—that is, the part that's after the @. In most cases, companies use only one domain name for all their email addresses. Which means, if the email address for Zero2Hired ends with @zero2hired.com, then it's most likely that John's email address ends with @zero2hired.com as well. That takes care of the domain, but what about what comes *before* the @?

This is where you can use trial and error with the three formats mentioned above. Do them one at a time and wait a minute or two between each. A bounce-back email means it didn't go through, so try the next format. If all three fail, then you're out of luck, my friend! But at least you gave it your best shot. IT departments of large organizations may also intentionally block any incoming emails from web-based email addresses such as Gmail or Yahoo.

This sneaky little tactic is courtesy of two authors who have worked in the IT industry for several years. It's not foolproof, but certainly has worked for most cases.

There are other sites that contain the contact information of individuals and the organizations they work for. These websites are primarily used to find leads for sales and marketing purposes. But these sites can also be utilized to meet the needs of job hunters. Some of our favourites are **http://www.zoominfo.com** and **https://connect.data.com.**

Zoominfo is a subscription-based service. Connect.data.com works on a points system—you update contact information to earn points that you can spend when you retrieve contacts. On these websites, you can find both email addresses and cellphone numbers (in case it comes down to making a phone call).

Now use your sleuthing skills to find the relevant people in your list for that job. Make note of their name and contact info, and maybe even their profile picture if you see it on LinkedIn—it's helpful to put a face to a name. Copy this information into your organization folder.

Step 5: Get personal with info

This is where you're going to shine compared to other applicants and one of the central points in this book. The details that you gather from this step are going to provide the bread and butter of your solution letter, so put your efforts into researching this information.

About the company: Google the company's name, and click on News to find out what the company has been up to. It could be expanding its premises or staff, launching a new product, starting a new initiative or winning an award. Any piece of information that you can muster should be added to your arsenal of personalization data that you will inject into your solution letter as the hook. You can also check the company on Facebook and LinkedIn to catch any updates posted there. Or just go directly to the company's website. Most organizations have a Press section.

About your contacts: Scout your contacts on LinkedIn. You have access to their complete profile and professional history, unless they have adjusted their security settings to hide it. Look for and note anything you have in common with them or that you can use to compliment them. You can even Google the contacts' names and see what comes up. Individuals may have also won awards and be mentioned in an article. If you have volunteered or been part of a community, you may also find that you have something in common with that person to use during the interview or in your solution letter.

About department challenges: The most useful details you can find are the challenges and problems the department you're applying to is facing. If you have experience in this field, you may already know the challenges faced by the hiring manager. If you're an emerging Millennial or an established Millennial changing careers, *when in doubt, Google it out:* "Challenges faced by... department" or "Challenges faced by... managers".

You may have another more promising option if you have a friend or family member working at the company you're targeting. This person may be able to do you a favour and introduce you to somebody who works in the department you are applying to. Remember, you don't need intricate details. Just a brief summary or outline of the broad challenges faced by the department would be enough to resonate with the hiring manager.

Step 6: Create your solution letter

It's time to combine your writing skills and personal research of public-facing online content to create a cover letter that will leave the employer yearning to open your resumé. People who have done their homework always impress.

Recall from chapter 4 that your solution letter has four parts: the hook, the problem, the solution and the proposal for contact. In the previous step, you researched personal information and here is where you will use it. If you like, revisit the solution letter section in chapter 4 where we described the solution letter creation process in detail, before you continue.

In the hook, use the specific info you dug up about the company and the person. The hook will make the reader interested in reading about what you have to say. That's the purpose of any hook. Ongoing company projects, awards it has won, awards the person has won, experience and qualifications about the person—anything that can be used to compliment your contact.

You then use the research you gathered on the challenges faced by the department to speak to the problem and solution sections of the letter. Here is where you empathize with the hiring manager on *one* challenge that he or she is facing in her department. Recall that the purpose of this letter is to hit a nerve, a pain point to get that manager thinking, "This person knows the problem I'm facing right now." And then you swoop in with a statement on how *you* are the solution to the problem. This can be either about the skills and knowledge you have to tackle the problem, or better yet, how you've solved this same problem in the past. But remember, *honesty above all.* Stating that you've solved it in the past is more effective, but don't fib if you haven't. Finally, you conclude with a proposal to make contact, where you propose to reach out to the manager directly to discuss if you're a good fit for the role. Using the examples from chapter 4, we've combined each section to give you an example of a solution letter below:

Dear Mr. Ribeiro,

I recently read that Zero2Hired won the award for **Best company for Millennials to work for** *6 years in a row now. You are a manager who has been working for the company for nearly 8 years, so I want to congratulate you for the leadership skills you bring to your teams, contributing to award-winning success.*

Accounts receivable plays a crucial role in ensuring a smooth cash flow to the company. As the manager, you must be accountable for strict targets being set by the finance management, and while you're busy dealing with customer relations and the sales team, you won't have the time to address the collection process yourself.

When I worked for XYZ Inc., 50 per cent of invoices were past their credit due date at the time I joined the company. As soon as I understood the policies and culture of the company and its customers, I worked closely with finance and sales to streamline the process and reduced our aged invoices to 8 per cent in 3 months.

I hope to have the chance to speak with you about the opening you have for an Accounts Receivable Specialist that I have applied for (JOB ID: #####). Please let me know when would be most suitable time for you, and I'll call you at that time.

Sincerely yours,

Connel Valentine

Note how you've stated at the end that you've already applied for the job, referencing the Job ID (if applicable). This is because you want to explicitly state that you've already followed the default process (coming up in step 7). Otherwise, if that person responds, the first question to you will be "Have you applied online?" With the statement about your application, you've already answered that question.

You need to create a different solution letter for each person you're connecting with. Remember, a senior manager or recruiter does not have the same problems as the hiring manager. You need to tweak your hook, problem and solution for those individuals. You can speak about the department problem and solution at a higher and more generic level, rather than a specific point that only the hiring manager would relate to. Or, even compliment the organization as a whole on its achievements and state the values and culture advertised on their website. As long as it's personal and customized, you're on the right path.

Step 7: Follow the rule book

First things first. You must apply for the job in the way the company expects you to. Apply for this position online or through the company's website, whichever is being asked. If you have to upload a file of your resumé, make sure it is in Microsoft Word format. *Do not upload files online in PDF format.* Some older versions of the application tracking system (ATS) cannot read PDF files well. Take note of the reference number that is generated, as you may be asked for it later. You can also add it to your solution letter and file. Remember to attach a solution letter to your formal application as well—use the solution letter directed at the *recruiter*, as it's most likely that your online application will be initially viewed by that individual.

Never apply for the same job multiple times. Not only does it suggest desperation, recruiters become annoyed and ticked off by it! Although you've submitted your application online, your process is far from over. The best description we've heard of the online application system is that it's a *black hole*. What goes in never comes out. You've carried out this activity as a formality because it's part of the process from the recruiter's perspective. It's out of the way now, and so... time to get down to business.

Step 8: Email your resumés

You are now going to take the first steps in reaching out to your contacts directly. Proudly armed with your customized and personalized solution letter and resumé, you will bypass the competition—the poor souls who think that their online submission will get them anywhere—and direct your resumé into the inbox of the people in charge of hiring you.

You've already researched the contacts and their email addresses and placed them into your organization folder. Now comes the task of emailing your resumé to those people. Note: Your solution letter should appear in the body of the email, while the resumé will be attached as a file. Although you had to upload your resumé as a Microsoft Word document online, we recommend using the PDF format for the direct email to your contacts. Adobe Reader is a common tool used in most offices, and it provides a clear, non-editable view of your resumé. As always, in your organizational folder be sure to make a note of the emails sent and responses received.

The subject line of the email is important because it's the first thing the reader sees. If the email is received on a mobile device (and these days there's a good chance of that happening), the display will initially only show the subject line. It would be great if your subject line is appealing or compelling enough to be opened rather than ignored. A subject line that just says "My Resumé" will most likely be ignored. A few of our recommendations include:

1. Your next Junior Accountant
2. Zero2Hired's newest Executive Assistant
3. A committed Data Entry Operator

The file name of your resumé would also add a professional touch. Instead of something that just says **resumé.pdf**, change the file name to your target job title like **Riley Lee - IT Services Team Leader.pdf**.

Send the email to the three players you've identified—the recruiter, likely hiring manager, and senior manager. If you believe there are more than three possible hiring managers from your LinkedIn search, send it to them as well. You lose nothing by doing this and have everything to gain.

Congratulations! You have now applied for a job in a way that will put you further ahead of the competition than you've ever been before! Admittedly, it's a long process, but as you apply for more jobs, we guarantee that it will become easier and faster for you. By your fourth or fifth application, you should be flying through the process.

Day 2

Step 1: Check your email

Depending on the time of day you sent your first email, you may or may not see a response just yet. You reasonably have to give people at least 24 hours to respond to an email. If you *do* get a response from one of the people you've selected, this is great news! It saves you from the jitters of making a cold call later.

The email response you receive could be one of the following:

1. Best case scenario, you've hit the jackpot and reached out to the hiring manager responsible for this position. The message you receive may tell you to apply for the position online (which you've already done).
2. You could also be asked to schedule a date and time for a phone or in-person interview. Or sometimes one of the recipients just picks up the phone and call you when you least expect it! If you've followed everything up to chapter 5, you are prepared for this call.
3. You could receive a response stating that the recipient is *not* the person hiring for this role, in which case you may be referred to the right person who is cc'd in the response. That serves the purpose too!
4. You could be told very bluntly *not* to email that person and waste his or her time. Hopefully you won't be reporting to this kind of manager.

Step 2: Respond to emails

First, start off with a quick note of appreciation, thanking the other person for responding to your email. (Just do this on the first response. You don't want to parrot your appreciation for every subsequent response.) Your own judgement and past experience should serve you well on how to respond to emails, but here are some guidelines for replying to the samples above.

Provide that person with the reference number that was generated when you applied for the position online. Continue by telling this person that you have a *keen interest* in the job, highlighting one of the key requirements in the job description, and then suggesting a phone interview. It could go something like this:

Hi Mr. Ribeiro. Thank you for taking the time to respond to my email. I have already applied for the position online, Ref No. 546TH54. I wanted to tell you in person how excited I am to apply for this position, as my prior experience in software development coding in Ajax fits perfectly with the requirements in the job description. I understand that personality also plays a key role for any candidate that you invest your time in, so I was hoping to have a phone interview with you at your earliest convenience. Will you be available in the afternoon on Tuesday or Wednesday?

Note that when giving a proposal for time or date, you *provide options* rather than leaving it open ended with something such as "Are you free any time?" Connel has personally found that this approach works pretty well. Beware: The more *open* you leave a response, the more likely the recipient is to *avoid* the commitment.

If you receive a response stating that the recipient is not the person hiring for this position and referring to somebody else, thank this person for the referral. Then direct your attention to the person they have introduced you to. The thank-you note should be sent in a separate email (with a *cc* to the person who is now being introduced) mentioning that you will deal directly with the new person. This gesture is highly appreciated by people in the office. Everyone complains about high email traffic, and your stating that you will exclude the person who is *not* concerned with the hire is an immediate show of professionalism and experience. It may sound something like this:

Hi Mr. Valentine. Thank you for taking the time to respond to the email. I appreciate the introduction. I'll reach out to Mr. Ribeiro directly in a separate email.

If you receive a harsh rejection, you can turn a rejection frown upside down. Apologize to the person for incorrectly reaching out to him or her, and ask if he or she would be so kind as to refer you to the right person. Some people like to hand things over to other people with an it's-your-problem-now attitude. It's not necessarily a bad thing, and sometimes there's a genuine reason. In this case, it works in your favour because you ultimately want to reach out to the right person to hire you. So, your response may sound something like this:

Hi Mr. Valentine. My apologies for directing my email to you. Would you happen to know the name of the person who is hiring for this position?

Don't take it to heart if you don't receive a response. Many individuals simply ignore emails that don't concern them. There are some, however, who feel the guilt of ignorance. And as blunt as they may be, you might just receive an answer from them that you can use. You'll never know until you ask!

Step 3: The call

If you've not received a response to any of your emails after 24 hours, the time has come to make the dreaded telephone call. We know that cold-calling someone would make most of you nervous. We have felt the same way. It's the fear of rejection, isn't it? You have to accept that rejection is possible and allow the increased chance of landing that new job to outweigh those fears. Sales people and telemarketers have this down to a science. They make cold-calls all the time and accept rejection as part of their job. Also bear in mind that what you may interpret as fear is quite simply *adrenaline,* which feels like fear. Learn to harness and accept that adrenaline rush and direct that energy into a positive call.

There are a few of details about people's behaviours that are worth mentioning here. As much as you fear rejection, most people are reluctant to be rude. There are some individuals who genuinely want to help you out, and some who don't. They don't want to be rude either. Here is where you can create leverage for yourself. Remember, the phone call does something that no resumé or online application can do—it gives the person at the other end an insight into your personality, which, as we mentioned before, is the most critical piece of the job application. If we have read and passed over a resumé that wasn't too impressive, but later received a phone call from this same person who seemed to have an engaging personality, it would convince us to give him or her a shot.

When you make a cold call, the more useful *leverageable* information you have, the more likely you are to positively connect with that person. With a weak and risky approach, you could say: *"Hi John. We've never spoken before, but I wanted to ask you about a job opening in your department."* You're on thin ice with this call. We don't recommend it. However, you could start your call this way: *"Hi John. I got your contact information from Connel, and he asked me to give you a call. It's regarding a position that's open in your department."* See what happened there? You used Connel's name as *leverage* to create a positive outcome for the conversation. Now in John's mind he's thinking "Okay, this person is not a *complete* stranger since Connel knows him too. Let's see what he has to say."

A referral call such as the one above is probably the most *powerful* form of leverage. You could also use other means of leverage, such as knowledge about the company, or a common interest you both share (that you dug up from the person's LinkedIn profile). Speaking of referral calls, if you can leverage a VIP's name on the call, that will surely grab attention for you. Just as your solution letter has a hook to grab the reader's attention, your cold call also needs a hook to keep the person interested in speaking with you.

As mentioned at the beginning of this chapter, VIPs are in an ironic situation—they are the *least* concerned with hiring you for the job, but also the ones who can give you the *most* leverage to get it. If you are to call somebody, consider start by making a respectful professional call to the VIP. You're actually *hoping* for that person to brush you off to somebody else, so you can use the VIP's name as leverage on the next call. Genius, eh?

New York Times bestselling author Martin Yate, in his book *Knock 'em Dead*, explains that having multiple goals in mind prior to engaging in a phone call will allow for multiple chances for success. Some of the goals you could create are:

1. to establish a date and time for an interview (best case scenario)
2. to establish a date and time to call the person back (if it's not a good time when you first call)
3. to be referred to somebody else in another *department* (if there aren't any opportunities in the department you called right now) or to be referred to somebody else in another *company* (if there aren't any opportunities in the entire company right now)
4. permission to send over a resume for subsequent follow-up

5. to keep the channels of communication open by receiving that person's *approval* to add him or her to your LinkedIn network (worst case scenario)

Every phone conversation you have provides opportunities for you to come away with at least one of the five outcomes above, in which case, the conversation worked in your favour.

Remember that as far as searching for work is concerned, one of our central themes in this book is getting personal and navigating your way to direct contact with the people who can hire you. Although it may terrify you to pick up the phone and speak to a manager or a director, remind yourself that you're doing this for your career and your future.

Practise! Practise! Practise! The best public speakers in the world still rehearse their speeches. The conversation you will have is no different. It's a speech about yourself with the potential for Q&A within it. Practise your introduction over and over again until it sounds natural. Try recording yourself on your phone. Hearing your own voice played back provides a whole new perspective about how you sound to other people. When you've perfected your introduction, practise what you'd say for each of the above five scenarios.

Here's a sample of how a conversation might go. There are five different possible questions that Mr. Ribeiro might have for your opening statement and a possible answer that you could have for each of them. Notice the technique of ending a sentence with a question to further the conversation.

You	"Good morning, Mr. Ribeiro. My name is Jane. We haven't spoken before, but Mr. Connel Valentine gave me your contact information. He also asked me to give you a call and to say Hi. I was hoping to have a few moments of your time to talk about the opening you have on your team for an IT Service Desk Analyst."
Response 1:	"Sure. Tell me about yourself."
Reply	"I have three years of experience working in the IT field, as the first point of contact for end users, resolving any issues from basic troubleshooting steps to more complicated problems that requires me to do research or consult with senior level engineers to resolve. I'm certified in ITIL and Comptia A+ and I'm willing to further my education in IT. I'm a firm believer in keeping my technical skills up to date. I know that Zero2Hired also values developing its employees, so I hope to be a part of the team and further develop my skills with you. Also, I'm familiar with challenges that service desks face to keep average handle times low and FCRs high, while also maintaining a high customer satisfaction score. I have successfully managed to do this and keep my statistics well above the targets set by the management. So, do these sound like skills that your department could use?"
Response 2:	"I'm not the right person to speak to. You'll have to speak to HR."
Reply	"That's sound good. Might I know whom I can get in touch with from HR?"
Response 3:	"I'm a little busy now, I have to get into a meeting."

Reply	"I understand. May I call you back later in the afternoon today or tomorrow at the same time?"
Response 4:	"That position's already been filled, and we don't have any more vacancies right now."
Reply	"I'm sorry to hear that. But in that case, can I get your opinion on my qualifications and experience so that I can know if I should keep an eye out for other opportunities in your organization." (If yes, then repeat your reply to response 1 above.)
Response 5:	"How did you get my number? We don't have any openings. Don't call me again."
Reply	"I researched your information online" (assuming this wasn't a referral call) "as I was eager to speak to you. I believe that I'm the perfect candidate for this role, and I'm really interested in working with Zero2Hired. If you don't have any openings now, may I add you on LinkedIn so we can keep in touch?"

Day 3

Mail your resumé

"Hold on! Mail?!?! As in, actual hard-copy documents? Real envelope-licking, stamp-thumping, mailbox-dropping *mail*? Who do you think I am, my grandmother?"

Now that we have all the frustration and shock out the way, yes, *mail your resumé*! How many people do you know who do this? Probably none.

All the more reason to do it if you want to *stand out* from the crowd and beat the competition.

Here's another way of looking at it. When a job is publicly advertised, how many people do you think are applying for it? Hundreds, right? What's the first thing you want when you apply to an advertised job? You'd want your resumé to be *opened* of course. Of those hundreds of resumés that were uploaded for that job, what percentage do you think were actually opened? The perfect candidate for that job was probably there all along, but this person's resumé was the proverbial needle in the haystack that was never opened in the first place. Sure, if the resumé contained the right keywords, the application tracking system may have brought it up to the top of the list. But why rely on the mechanics of a system to get your resumé opened, when you possess the power to make it happen yourself?

If your resumé is in an envelope that contains the person's name and address, it *will be opened*. No matter what. As long as you don't label the envelope with "This is my resumé, please read it!" your resumé will be opened. The mailing address is no secret, of course. As long as you know the office where the person is based (from the contact information you found earlier), you can Google the postal address of the office. Even if it does end up in the wrong branch, the company's internal mail personnel will redirect it to the right place. Have the person's name and office postal address on the envelope and nothing more. The recipient will not throw away unfamiliar mail in the trash without opening it first.

Connel received a call from an HR representative regarding a job he had applied for. She said to him, "I noticed you've been really interested in this job, with your snail mailing and all, so I thought I'd give you a call." Mission accomplished! However, she did tell him how it was unorthodox to do so, and probably not a good idea in the future. While he agreed out of courtesy, he thought to himself, "Whatever. It got you to see my resumé and call me, didn't it?"

If the emails and phone calls have gone unanswered and you don't have a single lead to follow for that job, buy large (i.e., 9 x 12) envelopes (so you don't have to fold your resumé) and stamps, and start mailing your resumé. Remember to print both the personalized solution letter, copied and pasted from the email you sent directly to the contact, along with resumé.

So, dear Millennial, while to you the concept of snail mail might be completely alien and Stone Aged, you must admit that the above benefit it provides makes sense. Statistically speaking, you've enormously increased your chances for an interview by taking steps to guarantee that your resumé will be viewed by the hiring manager. Bear in mind that it will take a couple of business days for your mail to reach its destination. They don't call it snail mail for nothing!

And that folks, is the first half of the job track process. It can take up to three days to launch and may continue for one to two weeks, depending on what follows. You may start a thread of emails with one of your contacts. You may even start a string of meaningful and fruitful conversations with some. Even better, the hiring manager may end up reading your mailed resumé after a couple of days and give you a call. And off you go to your interview!

Now, you might be thinking, *with this much effort for one job application, of course I'll be called for an interview, right?* Unfortunately, there is always the possibility that an application—no matter how amazing it is—will not yield an interview. Sadly, that's where the job track ends for that particular application. Don't be disheartened and certainly don't delete or pitch the organization folder. A lot of hard work went into learning about the organization's culture and values, discovering its leaders, and finding useful contact information. You never know, there could be another similar job posting in the not-so-distant future, and having done your research already, you may quickly find yourself very well prepared.

It's important to give your best efforts to every application you take on. And remember, we are aiming to shorten the time spent searching for work, not to nail every job you apply for.

So, you will repeat the above process for your subsequent job applications, keeping track of each one in an organization folder. Each application will gain different momentum in time.

The hidden job market

While the above job track process was initiated from an advertised job, the same process can also be used for the hidden job market. The only difference is that you will be using your generic resumé (since you don't have a job description to tailor it to).

Your initiator will be a target company that you want to work for rather than an advertised job. Once you've selected the company, you can kick off the same process from step 3 of day 1 and look for the key players in that company. The rest of the process of finding appropriate information, customizing your solution letter, emailing, calling and mailing your resumé remains the same.

Hitting the hidden job market with your direct emails and mailings is just as important as applying for an advertised job. You must therefore include it as part of your strategy. In this way, you are taking a more holistic approach to your job search, covering all your bases to seek advertised *and* unadvertised jobs.

Takeaways and exercises

So, this is how you reduce the overall amount of time you will spend looking for work. As you can see, the process is a job on its own, easily taking several hours per day of your time when you combine it with other networking activities. We will cover that later on. At first, you may find it challenging to mentally commit to such long hours, but this is no different from a real-life job. Once you find that target job, you will be dedicating nine to 10 hours per day (including commute time) to your job. This level of commitment should start from the day you start *looking*.

We'll admit it, the process is a lot more challenging for those of you who are already working and looking for a change. It will feel like having a second job. Nonetheless, the more hours you dedicate per day to it, the quicker you will start your new job and the next chapter in your career.

Finally, you are ready to start sending off your solution letters and resumés for both advertised jobs and the hidden job market possibilities within your target companies. While this process will already set you apart from the rest, in the next chapter we will take marketing your brand to the next level. You'll be leaving your competition behind in a cloud of dust!

CHAPTER 7

PERSONAL AND SOCIAL NETWORKING

Following the job track process may eventually become tedious (well, in some way we hope this happens because that means you've become skilled at the process). There are several other beneficial activities in which you should engage on a daily basis to vary your routine and avoid burning out. Remember, one of the key messages of this book is that job searching is a job in itself—and you can easily spend several hours per day doing it. This doesn't mean that you spend this much time just following the job track process. In this chapter, you will discover how to take your job search strategy to the next level and even further reduce the time you'll be searching for a job.

These days, it's well known that networking is a crucial activity in the development of your career. Many professionals claim that it's the *only* path to your next job. Networking can start at school, when you ask your professors for references or introductions to people they know for informational interviews. It continues even after you find a job, if you're smart. Creating job security isn't just about having a sure-fire job search tactic. It's also about being *known* in your industry to the people who have the authority to hire you when the time comes.

Networking is not about asking, "Can you please hire me." It's about marketing your brand—showing people what you have to offer and letting *them* decide that they need you when there's an opening. In this chapter, we'll explore the various ways to make your brand known to the world around you and how you can market your brand and propel yourself ahead of the competition.

But a word of caution: some of the methods shown here require a dose of courage. You may think to yourself *There is no way I can do that!* But yes, you *can* do it. Muster up the same courage you had when you paid your way through college, the same courage you had when you moved to a new country, the same courage you had when you passed your exams, and go for it! Nothing beats the power and value of networking in person. As connected as you may be to your smartphones and laptops, no job will be given to you just through an exchange of text messages. If reaching out to somebody directly intimidates you, this is one fear you *must* get over—for the sake of your career and your life!

Volunteering

The value of volunteering and providing community service has been taught in schools for as long as we can remember—and for a good reason. If you think that these initiatives stop at school, think again. Many professional organizations promote volunteering opportunities and encourage their staff to actively participate at social events and welcome the participation of others as well. The current organization we work for even gives staff members a day off to pursue volunteer work.

Volunteering gives you a true feeling of accomplishment along with commendation for providing selfless service to your community. As an added benefit, volunteering also provides a means to create career opportunities for yourself. If you are currently in school or just starting out and not participating in a volunteer program, you aren't doing either your community or your career justice. Perhaps you come from a different background where volunteering was not a cultural norm. In North America, taking an active role in your community by volunteering your services is something you need to start doing. Otherwise, you risk losing out on the opportunities it creates for those who are involved this way. According to the NSHSS 2016 Millennial Survey, 57 per cent of Millennials reported spending part of their free time volunteering. While it's refreshing to see the majority on board, nearly half of all Millennials are not reaping the benefits of volunteering. We hope to see those numbers climb higher.

When you volunteer your services, you are connecting with people you've never met before. They may be students or working professionals, and anyone you meet in this setting could have an opportunity up their sleeve, just waiting for the right moment (or person) to present it to.

John's stepson Julian is 16 years old and plays basketball in a league in Vaughan. Julian has always been passionate about basketball and school, and John is proud to see Julian so actively engaged in these important parts of his life. In December of 2014, organizers were looking for volunteers to help out a coaching program for younger kids. Julian stepped up. Not only was he eager to share his skills with the younger students, but as an added bonus, he also enjoyed hanging out with the program coordinators he worked with. This is no different from a real workplace environment—the people around you in an office play an important role in your development and contribute to your engagement in your work. Julian didn't know it, but he was learning how to work with others by reading body language, following instructions and shadowing a working professional who was in charge of the program.

Four months later, the program manager tapped Julian on the shoulder and asked "Do you have a Social Insurance Number?" He wanted to give Julian a job. When Julian asked what he would be required to do, the program manager replied, "Pretty much the same thing you're doing now, except I want to pay you." Julian has been doing this job for two years now. He spends three to four hours working at his job on weekend mornings and continues doing what he loves in the afternoon—playing ball!

There's an important moral to Julian's story. When he stepped up to volunteer at the age of 14, it was not a conscious decision made with the intent of getting work. The job happened on its own. And this development has been so inspiring for him that with the same selfless attitude, Julian volunteers and helps the Summer School camp coordinators. Julian is now confident that he can get a job with the camp organization if he chooses to.

Communities are built on the backs of volunteers, and the leaders of those communities began in the same way. These are successful people you'd want to associate with, to learn from and be mentored by, to help in your own path of successes. Volunteering almost guarantees that opportunities will present themselves to you, because someone is always watching. Just like in Julian's case, it's important to act as though no one is watching. Volunteer and contribute to your community with a selfless serving attitude the way Julian did, because it shows commitment to a task or project as well as your leadership capabilities. If it's meant to be, the person who's watching will come to you!

Where do I start?

In relation to your career, this is why volunteering can be of considerable help:

1. You may find volunteering opportunities connected to your field of work, in which case you benefit from first-hand experience with what the job can be like.

2. You benefit from significant exposure by meeting new people and showing off your winning personality to them

3. It's another feather in your cap when you've volunteered for an event that you could add into your LinkedIn profile. Employers would be pleased to know that you make a contribution to the community by volunteering your time.

If you are an emerging Millennial, you're probably already familiar with volunteering and community involvement, as schools have made such activities mandatory. Here are some sources for finding volunteer opportunities:

1. **Volunteertoronto.ca** is a great place to start for Ontarians. You can filter your volunteer opportunities by many categories, including professional fields. For example, selecting IT support as a category yields many volunteer opportunities for IT support assistance and developers, for example.

2. Some of the larger companies that you want to target may offer volunteering opportunities. Google "open volunteering

opportunities with *ABC Company*". You will find a host of opportunities with many of the major companies.

3. Googling for volunteer opportunities in your state or province will provide you with a variety of choices to be part of a program where you can network your way to a successful career. *When in doubt, Google it out.*

Now there are a few dos and don'ts to keep in mind when you are participating at a volunteering program. Running around asking everybody for their business cards and inquiring about job opportunities is *not* going to help you. In fact, hustling for interviews will not impress anybody and will make the people you want to impress question your motives for volunteering in the first place. By no means should you use the volunteer event to talk with *anyone* about getting a job. The jobs will come. For now, you are at this event to be energetic, to participate, to be positive and to make a difference. By volunteering you will be noticed, and somebody is always watching. By all means, engage and talk to people about the event and about social topics. Share a laugh while you're doing the community work and establish a positive relationship with your cohorts.

Once the dust has settled on a big, one-time or annual event, you can ask for the full name and company those other volunteers work for, so you can find them later on LinkedIn. Keep in touch and *then* start the professional talk.

John volunteered at a Toastmasters Convention in Washington as well as at several other public speaking events. He has crafted certain rules and personal values that he follows while at these events. These rules cover everything from how to meet and greet new people to the principles of establishing lasting relationships with them.

Here is a list of dos and don'ts that we've recognized when volunteering and networking at special events.

DO ☺	DON'T ☹
Participate in the event as required. Go above and beyond when you can.	Ask for business cards or job interviews.
Be positive, energetic and focused. Make it seem as though you want to be there.	Be on your phone trying to catch up on Facebook or Twitter.
Lend a helping hand to anyone who asks for it.	Show up late or leave early.
Be willing to get your hands dirty for the good of the event.	Have a negative attitude or act like you're doing everyone a favour by being there.
Continue staying in contact via LinkedIn or Twitter.	Consider any task menial and shy away from it.

Volunteering opportunities may last from a single day up to several days. Before the end of the program, it's important to keep in touch with any professional contacts with whom you've developed a positive relationship. Don't ask for phone numbers, as that may seem too pushy. But you do want to keep in touch on LinkedIn to continue fostering your relationship. More on this coming up.

Professional Communities

For any field in which you might like to work, there should be a professional community out there where other like-minded professionals with similar skills and interests meet to collaborate in their respective fields. These organizations present both networking and learning opportunities. You should seek them out and become an active participant. Not only will you surround yourself with enthusiasts who bring new ideas and support your career, but you will also start to strengthen your own job security by networking with people in the same industry as yours who are connected with the job market in which you specialize. It's LinkedIn on steroids—direct networking with people in your area and in your field of expertise.

Public speaking is one of John's passions, and he's part of the one of the most exclusive Toastmasters club in downtown Toronto. Although most Toastmasters clubs generally welcome newcomers into their community, this particular club only accepts the most committed and highly skilled speakers. Through this club, John has connected with extremely experienced and motivated people whose ambition is infectious. Some have authored books, hosted workshops or organized community events. Some members have even left the club because they could not keep up to the level of commitment that this club gives to the community. By continuing to challenge himself and persist with relentless commitment to this organization, John is now in a position where he's created his own job security through this organization. He knows that any time he needs them—whether he's out of work or interested in becoming an entrepreneur—he has the complete support and guidance of these colleagues.

When in doubt, Google it out! There are communities out there for every field that interests you, and if you have access to a thriving business hub like Toronto, you should be able to Google these communities. Individual local clubs are sometimes also referred to as chapters. Just type in, for example, "mechanical engineering communities in Toronto (or Montreal or Vancouver)." Some of these communities may charge a fee, so look into all the details and reviews on them. Connect with members on LinkedIn or Facebook for first-hand insight on what the community is like. Those who participate in these communities have one thing in common—they all take their field of expertise very seriously, and when a job opening becomes available, their own community is a potential and *trusted* source for hiring. One notable resource for finding these types of groups is **meetup.com**.

Informational interviews

Social network websites are wonderful, but their limitation is right there in their description—they are *online* websites. Hiring only happens after a face-to-face interaction with someone. No one is going to hire you from your LinkedIn profile alone or from texting. Meeting people in a one-on-one setting is an important part of the job hunt process, and it does not mean meeting people only with a can-you-get-me-a-job attitude.

Some meetings are purely for informational purposes. Ultimately, everybody knows someone who knows someone. Now, the thought of reaching out to a total stranger may scare you. You may also be thinking *Why would this person want to meet up with me? What's in it for them?* First, if you are introduced through another person who will act as the bridge in your interaction, you won't be a *total* stranger because you have a referral from a common friend or acquaintance. Secondly, people *love* to talk about themselves, especially if they have established careers. It's human nature. When you go on a date, what's the general rule? Ask the *other* person about himself or herself. Similarly, when you reach out to someone to have an informational meeting, make sure that what you're asking is to be enlightened on *that person's* experiences.

Don't make it sound as though you're asking the person to carry out a task for you, for example by asking, "Can you look through my resumé to see if I'd be hirable?" That's work and effort that people are naturally resistant to. However, if you frame your request like this:

> *"Hi Connel. We have a common friend John and he told me you would be the best person to speak to about advice in the IT Industry. I hope he gave you a heads up that I'd be calling you. I wanted to know if you'd be free for a coffee on Wednesday or Thursday afternoon. I was hoping you'd share your past experiences in the IT field and the challenges you faced in your career, as I'm interested in the field myself."*

Notice how the request makes it all about the other person? This will draw the person in: "Talk about my career? Sure, no problem!" And with a little luck, you've got yourself an informational interview. You may recall, we used a similar strategy when creating a solution letter.

Remember to prepare any questions you have beforehand and take notes so that the other person knows that you're taking his or her time and effort to meet with you *seriously*. Some questions you could have are:

1. What *challenges* have you faced in your career?
2. What type of *personalities* have you come across that you admire?
3. What *types of companies* have you worked for, and how have they affected your career?
4. What does a *typical career path* look like for someone in your position?
5. What are the most *common problems* faced by the management of this profession or industry?

If you're just starting off on your career or changing career lines, this information is invaluable. At the very least, it serves to validate what you have on your resumé as well. The person you're speaking to is a subject matter expert in the industry that you both share (or that you are trying to join), and he or she may uncover a specific problem faced in the industry that could be useful to add in your resumé or solution letter.

The meeting should conclude with a vital piece of information:

> *"Thanks for meeting with me, Connel. I really appreciate you taking the time to meet with me and share your knowledge and expertise. I'm really drawn to this field and want to learn more about it. Do you know anyone else I can get in touch with and ask for their advice?"*

You come away with yet another person you can reach out to at a later date. Before trying to contact to the new person, always make sure that either you have been introduced or the new person has received a heads-up (from the colleague). That way, you're not a total stranger, so the new person will be more comfortable to meet with you.

So, what do you take away from meeting people for informational interviews? First, it's a chance to take a break from the job track. Second, you're speaking to someone with a common interest in your professional industry. You will enjoy the conversation and may have valuable updates for your resumé and LinkedIn profile. Third, this person is aware of your existence (in case an opportunity occurs in their world), and has provided the contact information of another person for you to network with.

Also, if this person is a hiring manager or knows a hiring manager, you've literally engaged in a pre-screening process that an HR person would normally do before calling you in for an interview. This person has now experienced your personality first hand and, regardless of your experience and qualifications, you will come to mind if that person hears of an opportunity through his or her network.

Always come away with that person's business card, add this new contact to your LinkedIn, and with his or her acceptance of the connection, send a message to express your sincere thanks for his or her time… and *keep in touch*! It's the least you can do to return the favour. Keep periodically reaching out to these contacts on LinkedIn, just to say Hi, or to share an update about your job search or something you read online that could be of interest. This way, these contacts are always reminded of your existence out there. More on LinkedIn management coming up.

Co-ops and internships

If you are early in your career, or better yet, still in school, co-ops and internships offer extremely powerful insight into the job market and the industry. A lot of large enterprises like the one we work in have graduate programs and internship programs. The participants of these programs receive real-world experience and an enhanced knowledge of the way that particular fields of business works. Take these opportunities when you can, as early as possible. Although they may pay very little or nothing, they are ideal for you to expose your brand to the professional world.

You may be concerned that taking on co-op programs and internships would extend your graduation date. This is true. You may also be telling yourself *If I'm doing nothing but studying and working all year, I'll probably only get two or three weeks off per year.* Welcome to the corporate workforce. If real-life working experience is your objective, then this is to be expected. Once you are employed, two or three weeks per year is the typical vacation time you can expect to have when you are starting off. A publication from Statistics Canada (**statcan.gc.ca**) reveals that students who complete co-ops report a better job-to-education match and higher earnings than those who do not complete a co-op. If co-ops and internships are not in your list of goals to pursue, we seriously ask you to reconsider. Put yourself in the position of a hiring manager who has the option of selecting a candidate with no experience in the field versus a candidate with some experience through these programs. Which would you choose?

A Google search on co-op and internship opportunities will show you the availability of jobs as well as the company that's hiring. The job track process applies to these applications as well.

A word of caution, though. If you are currently in an intern program (especially an unpaid one), don't sacrifice momentum on your job track process. There's only so long you can work for free or for minimal pay. At some point, you must find a secure job that can pay the bills. Keep following your job track process and keep networking. Be aware that it will be harder if you are dedicating time toward your internship, but hopefully this won't be for too long.

Online social networking

Now that we've covered how to network in person, let's move on to something that's more your comfort zone—the digital world. Before we discuss the various social networking sites, make sure you have set up your Google Alerts at **http://www.google.com/alerts**, as discussed in chapter 3.

These alerts give you frequent doses of information that you can use in your networking community or industry. You will be using this information to reach out to your Twitter followers and your LinkedIn connections.

You'll receive alerts about articles, blogs, news headlines, etc. with useful information. Successful people keep themselves well informed. They appreciate the importance of learning and being in the know. They will certainly appreciate new information from an article that you've uncovered. Or, it could just be something thought-provoking or compelling you read that you might direct as a question to someone.

Google Alerts essentially presents an easy opportunity to reach out to your social network.

Social media has now influenced the hiring process across the board. In July 2016, a Jobvite survey of 1,600 recruitment and HR professionals revealed that 87 per cent use LinkedIn, 43 per cent use Facebook (that's right!) and 22 per cent use Twitter to scope potential candidates for the hire. Surprised to see Facebook and Twitter rank so high? More on that coming up.

Keeping LinkedIn energized

LinkedIn likes it when you're active on it. The more active you are on LinkedIn, the more likely you are to turn up in search results when employers look for people based on specific criteria. You can always *pay* your way into this privilege with a Premier account. Still, being a frequent LinkedIn user helps bring your professional persona to light in the online professional world.

There are several things you can do during your day to boost your LinkedIn visibility

Manage your LinkedIn connections

If you're new to LinkedIn and have just created a profile, start adding connections. The obvious place to start will be friends and family, but you can also expand to former co-workers or people you met while volunteering or doing part-time jobs.

There is one very important note here: Unlike other social networking sites that you use, LinkedIn is *not* a popularity contest. Having more connections on LinkedIn is not necessarily an advantage. Our recommendation is to ensure you only add people who you will commit to connecting with on a fairly regular basis (more on this later). Friends and family and coworkers are an exception, you've already have a pre-existing relationship with them, and they will never forget you. But for other connections, you want to be sure that you will reach out to them regularly to keep in touch and let them know you still exist. Otherwise, they serve no purpose for being on your list. The information you receive from Google Alerts is one option for conversation starters. Remember to establish deeper connections, rather than developing a wider reach.

> Connel schedules time in the month to reach out to his contacts in his LinkedIn profile with questions, comments and likes. For his influential contacts, he shares updates and articles that he's read online about their particular line of work. He has even gone so far as to start *removing* connections from his LinkedIn profile to focus his efforts. Oddly enough, this activity actually started *increasing* his profile views. As for friends and family and former co-workers, he knows that he has already established a trusting relationship with them for networking purposes. Of course, he still gives them a shout on birthdays, promotions and other special occasions.

Get personal and touch base with your connections

What's the point of having people on your connection list if they don't know you exist? As always, the "get personal" rule still applies. Before reaching out to your contacts, check their profile for their qualifications or find some latest news from their company, and send them a message. Here's an example:

> *"Hi John, hope you're keeping well. I see that Zero2Hired is going through an expansion in Europe. They've also introduced a new technology that automates scripting. I hope you're getting to use your PMP expertise on these projects. Have a great week ahead and keep in touch!"*

It's smart to reach out and let people know you're alive. That's one of the whole points of networking, isn't it? The person receiving the message may just give your profile a quick look. In the event of any openings, you may well hear from that person.

This is where Google Alerts can also be used. When you've added someone new to your network, research the company they work for and set up an alert in their field or industry. This gives you another opportunity to reach to them. *"Hi Connel. I came across this article you might be interested in. Here's the link…"*

Join groups, follow channels, share and like information

We're sure you're already familiar with this. Just as you would do for your personal social network sites, you can also join groups and *like* or *share* various articles and images posted by individuals in your network. It's important to understand, however, that LinkedIn is dedicated to professional content only. This means it'd be best to leave shares about pets and food to Facebook, and focus on shares about your professional industry to LinkedIn.

Write your own posts

Attention bloggers! This is a great way for an employer to see what you're made of. Select any professional topic that you can write about, and create a post. Make sure it's been thoroughly proofread before posting, because it will show up on your profile and employers may look at it.

Again, keep the topic professional and related to your area of expertise only. If you're an IT professional, you can write about the benefits of the latest version of Windows, helpful tips for Java scripting, best practices for database structures, etc.

Twitter

Twitter has been gaining immense popularity in the professional world. Companies are now posting updates not just to promote their brand and products, but even to advertise job vacancies. For example, @toronto-jobs and @tojobs show various vacancies that are available in Toronto.

From a networking perspective, Twitter has one major benefit over LinkedIn. It allows you to send a 140-character message directly to anyone. When managers receive random requests to connect on LinkedIn, they are always skeptical. We never accept LinkedIn requests from people we have never met or interacted with before. However, Twitter allows you to reach out to people without a prior connection acceptance. This gives you an opportunity to introduce yourself before going via the LinkedIn route.

The easiest introduction to somebody you want to connect with is by offering value. Use Google Alerts to find any newsworthy article on an industry and tweet it directly to the person you want to connect with. Adding a personal message such as *"I checked out your LinkedIn profile and thought this article might interest you because of your expertise in..."* After this, you have much more leverage to make that LinkedIn contact and get an Accept.

By following people in your industry and committing to sending out at least one or two tweets per day, you make yourself known among the people in your industry who are in the Twittersphere, so you can network with them. You can even set up informational interviews or ask for community gathering info from these folks.

Facebook

You might be under the impression that Facebook is used for personal social networking. That is where Facebook established its roots back in 2004 when it became popular. Now, Facebook is starting to step into the professional realm as well. Companies have established groups on Facebook for promoting their brand and even for hiring. The 2016 survey by Jobvite shows that 43 per cent of recruiters use Facebook to scout for new hires. If you have target companies or industries, following these groups will give you insights on what's been happening at the company that you can leverage for communicating with your network.

Because Facebook will have a footprint into your personal life, you must be extra cautious about what your Facebook account reveals, starting with your photos. If cleaning up your Facebook pictures is not something you want to do, at the very least start securing those pictures with your privacy settings. If you're going to be adding professional people such as work colleagues to your Facebook network, create a separate professional group list for them and be sure to share only professional material with them.

The advantage that Facebook has over LinkedIn and Twitter is its popularity. Secure your professional network with a combination of privacy settings and lists *(Google it out to know how)* and you can leverage your brand on Facebook too, just as you would with LinkedIn and Twitter. Share professional articles, posts and blogs with your professional group on Facebook. Don't forget to update the Work and Education sections of your profile.

As tempting as it may be, never ask for jobs on social media. Your goal is to always provide value first and network with your contacts second.

Creating your online resumé

Here is where you set yourself apart form the crowd in a big way. What do all brands have in common? They all have a website to market and explain what their brand is all about. You are a brand—your beliefs, strengths and impact are unique to you alone. As such, your brand needs to be marketed online.

Taking your resumé online allows you to create an image for yourself like no other social media site can do. It will also create a unique impact on the hiring manager that no other site can do. The website you create will be completely designed by you, so everything about *who you are* and *what you've done* can be marketed on this site.

Creating a website is not difficult anymore—you literally just point and click or drag and drop. Common online services that provide this are **Wordpress.com** and **Wix.com**.

Place your professional picture front and centre, start blogging on your site, create a digital and downloadable copy of your resumé and post videos—yes, *videos* of yourself talking about what you have to offer. Hiring managers don't know what they are missing because they have never met you or seen your work in action. Your online resumé will give them insights into your professional brand before they even meet you. If your website is designed well enough, the interview could just be a formality to them.

Creating your website is a big step that takes your job application process to the next level—this is why we call it an *upgrade*. Setting up your own domain name with hosting services is extremely affordable. Many website design sites show you how, or you can view demos on YouTube.

To get you started, have a look at Connel's online resumé that he created using Wix:

http://www.connelvalentineresume.com

Having your own website allows you to present your professional self in a new light to the hiring manager. You can literally show off your talents and creativity and think-outside-the-box attitude. Your link will be an integral part of your brand and will follow you wherever your professional persona is marketed, including your own resumé and LinkedIn profile. If you have an online resumé, be sure to mention it in your solution letter and on your LinkedIn profile as well.

Advertise your brand

We're not done yet! Here, we are going after the hidden job market by handing your brand to the hiring managers. The higher up the manager is, the more authority that person has to even *create* a position for you.

Recruiters and hiring managers alike want talented employees in their organization. But unlike recruiters, hiring managers can spot talent beyond the job description, simply because they are the subject matter experts on how their departments operate. They are aware of *pockets of pain points* in their operation that can be filled by someone with unique talents.

For example, there may be an advertised position for a software developer for which case the recruiter would narrow the focus on the skills and experience being asked of such a role. Meanwhile, the hiring manager could come across a resumé of someone not so skilled in software development but with an impressive track record demonstrating proficiency with numbers—this just might lead to the creation of a business intelligence role for this person. Why? Although the recruiter doesn't know this, the manager answers to his senior management with data analytics and reporting on the department's progress. Alternatively, this manager may know of another team that could really use someone with a skill for numbers.

Think outside the box

We have read fascinating articles about creative and courageous individuals who, unafraid of putting themselves out there, launched a bold strategy to advertise their brand.

In one example, an individual designed his online resumé to look like Amazon's web page. He had over a million hits to his resumé and received multiple job offers.

Another individual took out Google ads geared to top directors of various advertising agencies. He then used these as the hook in his cover letter to those directors, that if they Googled their own names, the first thing they'd see was an ad of him asking them for a job.

But by far, the most effective and simplistic campaign we have come across is someone who created an online resumé and took out specifically targeted Facebook ads in which he specified the name of a specific company of interest to him. Everyone on Facebook whose profile indicated that they worked for those companies saw his ad. In a span of two weeks he was called for five interviews. Others tried the same tactic and were able to gain both information and leads to important contacts. Based on these people's experiences, it is suggested that you target one company or industry per ad (along with geographic filters) so you can address that specific company in your message.

If you've got the guts to take bold steps such as these, or better yet, get your creative juices flowing and come up with your own ad campaign for your brand, go for it!

Takeaways and exercises

Well, we've covered a lot of new ground here, and you've been enlightened on how job searching can take up a considerable portion of your day. In-person networking is by far the most effective way to be noticed and expose your brand. This is done through volunteering, joining communities, informational interviews, co-ops and internships.

Exercise:

Google for these professional community and volunteering opportunities around town, using sites like meetup.com or volunteertoronto.ca. Start attending these events.

Also reach out to the people in your network to arrange for informational interviews to gather more insight on your current industry or the industry you want to make a change to.

Talking to strangers in an informal setting will also help you practice for the formal interview later on.

We then moved to the digital world and covered keeping LinkedIn energized as a daily activity and paying attention to your online footprint with Facebook and Twitter. Pushing your brand to the next level by creating your very own online resumé or personal website and blogging from it will really distinguish you—especially if you decide to share those blogs on LinkedIn to drive more traffic to your site.

Exercises:

1. Update your LinkedIn profile, pare down your network and start connecting with the remaining people.
2. Start using Google Alerts to provide appropriate conversation starters.
3. If you feel ready, start working on that online resumé.

Before closing the discussion on networking, we suggest that you Google *yourself*. Surveys show that recruiters have refrained from hiring certain candidates because of the footprints they had left online—either a questionable photograph or a comment that's written in bad taste. In addition, a hiring manager may consider what is found online as part of your background check, which is a defining factor in the hiring process.

Exercise:

Give your online footprint a scan by Googling your name and seeing what comes up. Clean up anything that you wouldn't want a hiring manager or recruiter to find, including Facebook photos (adjustable in your security settings) or any blogs, written reviews or videos that you might have posted.

We have now completed what can be done to get noticed, stand out in the crowd and snatch up those interviews. We know it's a lot to take in. Your job search strategy thus far may have been to spend an hour a day online tossing resumés into the application tracking system black hole, then spending the rest of the day kicking back with your friends. If so, the switch to following these guidelines is going to be a huge change for you.

As an older Millennial, Connel has learned one poignant lesson about his professional life: He will never get back the time in his early 20s that he spent partying, playing videos games and socializing. And the real kicker, a little too much focus on these activities slowed down his career progression. That said, Connel does not condone being a workaholic—because time spent with friends and family is essential to our well-being. But in the past, he did not balance his career and his social entertainment well enough to achieve the career that he could have already had today.

Because of the ongoing and fantastic developments in the technology that surrounds us, instant gratification has become engrained in all of us.

Yet, career success *cannot* be achieved by a click on Amazon or Netflix. Building a career takes *time, effort* and *hard work*. The earlier you decide to dedicate your time to it, the earlier in life you will reap the rewards. Don't let Mark Zuckerberg's youth fool you—according to several blogs and articles, while his friends were out partying, he would stay in his dorm room and work on coding his website until the early hours of the morning.

Networking takes time. It will require months and maybe even years to establish a network that you can rely on for job security. If you're an emerging Millennial just out of school, *start now!* If you are an established Millennial already in the workforce, it's never too late. We know that the 9-to-5 job combined with the commute is physically and mentally taxing to begin with, but the directors and VPs in your department were once in the same position as you are now. These successful people had the same 24 hours in the day, but through their hard work, dedication and careful priority setting, they patiently networked their way to the top. On that note, it's now time to get you ready for your interview.

CHAPTER 8

PREPPING FOR THE INTERVIEW

Reaching out to people directly, getting personal with your solution letter, creating a conversational resumé that speaks to a hiring manager's problem, and using a persistent, methodological approach to the job hunt has inevitably paid off—you have an interview!

This is where the jitters and nerves start to kick in. Remember, it's not fear, but just *adrenaline* that must be harnessed to performance. The secret? It happens with thorough preparation. This chapter focuses on the eight steps you must do to properly prepare for the upcoming interview. You only have one shot at it—second chances are extremely rare. Even though it wouldn't be the end of the world if you didn't get the job, you're not doing your career justice if you don't give your all at every interview.

1. Review the job description

If this is a publicly advertised position, you have the details safely filed away in your organization folder. Review the job description carefully and contemplate the details of your past experience. Use your knowledge base file as a guide. Think about the challenges that could be faced in this role and prepare to address them. This exercise will allow you to answer the question *What do you know about this job position that we are offering?*

2. Review the company

Usually, you will be asked what you know about the organization, especially if you're interviewing for a small or medium-sized company. To prepare, review the high-level major points about the company from its website and from Google News articles that pop up.

At the very least, you should know the following five pieces of information:

1. The industry that the company is in (oil, technology, finance, event management, etc.)
2. The flagship product; for a small-medium size business in the technology industry, for example, what is the main product currently being distributed. For a company in the service industry, (such as event management, tourism, marketing, accounting, etc.), what is its core service. (The event management firm may specialize in weddings or corporate events, for example.)
3. What makes its flagship product or service *different*, and who are their competitors?
4. What is the size of the company in terms of staff strength, and where are its geographical locations?

5. Based on current news articles, what are the trends and updates from this company? These could include a major expansion, a new product launch, or even an award for a recent accomplishment.

3. Rehearse your interview questions

You created a knowledge base from the stories from your past and present to be used as a resource to answer majority of interview questions in chapter 5. Now your preparation pays off.

Exercise:

Review your knowledge base notes over and over again to be ready for your interview.

If you have a friend who's willing to help, ask that friend to play the role of the interviewer using the questions for which you've prepared responses. Then ask that 'interviewer' to evaluate your performance.

This should be a fun exercise, but keep an open mind and request honest feedback (meaning good *and* bad comments) from your friend.

If you have a relative who also happens to be a hiring manager, that person's opinions will be of further value.

You can also record your own answers on your cellphone and play them back. Remember, it's a whole new perspective to hear you own voice the way the interviewer will hear you. You should *not* be reciting your answers from rote memory or reading from a piece of paper (or your cellphone!) This must have the flow of a natural dialogue—you capture the key points about your answer and talk it through.

For each interview, there will be new questions to prepare for—those with answers that must be specific to the role and company for which you are interviewing. Once you've updated your research on the company and reviewed the job title and description, complete the following exercise.

Exercise:

Prepare answers to the following questions:

> *Tell me about yourself?* We know you've already prepared for this question, but if you remember the contents of this answer from chapter 5, part of it is speaking to your strengths and beliefs and supporting it with a story. Based on the company and the job description you are now reviewing, you may want to speak to different strengths and beliefs. For example, if you notice an obvious focus on communication skills, use that strength and story from your pool of knowledge in your introduction.

> *Why do you want to work for our company?* You could make a reference to the company's products, or any awards or projects that you have read about online.

> *What do you know about this job?* Give a brief summary of the job description and a reference to a problem that your role would solve.

4. Prepare your final questions

During the interview process, the interviewer will be introducing the company, explaining the purposes of the role you're applying for and other general information. This will undoubtedly answer several of the questions you have with regard to the job and the company. But inevitably, some questions are left unanswered, so at the end you will always be asked, "Do you have any questions for me?" All interviews, whether on the phone or in person, whether it's round 1 or round 10, will end with this question. *The wrong answer to this question is "No!"* You should always have a question at the end, no matter what. It's human nature to interpret the asking of questions as a person's interest. *You must give the impression to the interviewer that you are interested in the job.*

Based on the review of the job description and the company, you will have to ask intelligent questions at the end of the interview. By intelligent, we mean questions that relate to the company and the department and to the requirements and challenges that will be faced in the position you are trying to fill.

There are some standard questions that you could ask at the end.

1. What's the company's culture like?
2. What challenges will I face in this role?
3. What projects will I be tackling, if any, in the first year of the job?
4. What type of person would succeed in this role?

Do not ask about:

1. Pay, benefits and perks
2. Disadvantages of the company or department
3. Difficult people or situations
4. The future of this job

Stay clear away from questions regarding salary and benefits in the interview. These questions have a time and place *after* you have received the job offer. At most, you will be asked for the approximate range of your salary expectations, but the negotiations will happen later. This will be covered in the next chapter.

Of course, ask positive questions about the company. There are *always* difficult individuals in any given department, and you will have to deal with them as professionally as possible. It's a given, so don't ask.

You may also think about asking what the future holds for this position, thinking that this displays ambition. *As a general rule, don't focus on anything other than what the current position is asking, because that is what you're interviewing for.* 'Thin ice' questions can make the interviewer think that the first thing you'd want to do after getting the job would be to find the path to better ones in other departments or even other companies. (In the interviewer's mind, Millennials are notorious for this.). Stick to what the interviewer needs right now for *this* position. Any prospects of the future will be brought up by the interviewer with the question, "Where do you see yourself in five years?" That will be your queue to (carefully) talk about the future. Other than that, stick to the facts in the present.

> We once interviewed a candidate for a short-term contract and were sold at the end of the interview by the question she asked. As always, we asked the candidate if she had any questions for us. She began, *"Yes, I understand that this role is only for a short period of three months."* Pause. In our minds, we knew what was coming next. We'd heard it many times before. Either it was going to be a question about the possibility of extending the contract, or the possibility of this becoming a full-time role. Instead, the question was *"Since the contract is for such a short duration, will the training period be compromised or will I receive the full level of training like everyone else?"* Right there, was the reason the job offer was extended to her the very same day! It showed that she was *focused on the job at hand* and getting it done to the best of her ability—over her personal needs in the future. It showed that learning was an integral part of her personality and career development. This candidate's priority wasn't her situation at the end of her contract, but what she'd need to do *now* to learn her job tasks, get on her feet and get the job done. What character!

5. Review the salary range

You will eventually be asked about your salary expectations. You may also commonly see this ask in the job application itself. It's important to find the *market value* of the position you're applying for, because it's *likely* (but not guaranteed) that the company will offer the same.

Exercise:

Start a Google search with "average salary for …" where you type in the title of the job you are applying for.

Also visit **http://www.payscale.com** (our favourite source for the market values of job titles).

As mentioned in chapter 3, other popular sites are Glassdoor and even LinkedIn. You will most certainly see a range from these websites, and when preparing to answer this question, *have a range in mind.*

In reality, a budget has already been decided for this position, but the company won't tell you the real value. From the company's perspective, costs should be kept as low as possible. This does not mean, of course, that the candidate with the cheapest expectations will get the job. We urge you, please do not undervalue yourself by asking for a lower pay. As long as your desired salary figure is within range of the company's budget, the candidate with the *best cultural fit* and *personality* will get the job—even if that person is more expensive (but within budget) than another candidate.

There is another important concept to keep in mind, especially when working for large enterprise companies. The salary amount you agree on will be an anchor for the rest of your career with that company. In many organizations, HR has a policy on salary increases, and it's calculated based on a percentage of your existing pay. For example, the policy may state that annual increases cannot increase more than 3 per cent of your existing pay per year, and promotions may not result in a pay increase of more than 8 per cent of your existing pay. They may also have a grading system in place for all positions in the company that aligns to salary.

Either way, you can see why your *starting* salary is an important factor to consider, as your annual increases, bonuses and promotional increases will always tie back into it. So, this is why we repeat, *never* compromise your starting pay out of desperation to get the job. You will regret it at some point, as you wonder why the new person sitting next to you and doing the same job is making more than you are.

6. Prepare sample work and documents

At times, there is value in bringing in any work you have done in the past, *assuming it's unique and relevant to the job.* Software developers and programmers are good examples. Their work can be demonstrated to the interviewer on a laptop, along with a supportive dialogue about their values of how they went about creating this work. This show-and-tell opportunity can really leave a great impression with the interviewer. With the many applicants they will interview for the position, a visual aid leaves a more lasting and memorable impression.

Please remember, however, that if you are currently in the work force and want to show off your past work, you must consult your current company's information security policies or any other applicable policies. Anything you create under the payroll of a company may legally be owned by them, and these policies may prevent you from exposing this work to other organizations, especially the competition.

Remember to take one or two printed copies of your resumé along with a print-out of your references. Although the interviewer will have a copy of your resumé, less-skilled interviewers may clumsily waste time digging around for it. Having a copy that you can offer is another opportunity to demonstrate your preparedness. In most cases, you have not been asked for references prior to the interview. If the interviewer asks for them, you are ready with a list of references in your hand.

7. Know the logistics

To summarize the travel part of preparing for your interview, remember the following:

> 1. Put your outfit together the previous day. The last thing you'd want is to spot a stain on your interview outfit as you are getting dressed for the interview, forcing you to settle for something that's second best from your closet.
> 2. Location. Location. Location. Triple-check the address and use Google Maps to determine how long it will take to get there. Aim to leave earlier, in case something unexpected occurs (traffic, weather delays, etc.). It's also a good idea to have a phone number to call (but *only* in the event that you are going to be delayed). If you are using public transport to get there, it could work in your favour. Although the trip may take longer, you won't need to worry about parking.
> 3. Plan to arrive at least 15 minutes in advance, to shake off the commute and to prepare for what lies ahead.

Special Note to Smokers: On the day of the interview, it's best to avoid the cigarettes until it's behind you. The scent of tobacco smoke should not accompany you into the interview room. Jitters and nerves will tempt you to reach for a cigarette, but muster up the self-discipline just this once before the interview. As the smoking public is now a minority, consider the possibility that your interviewer is *not* a smoker. You already know that non-smokers are put off by the smell of tobacco.

Takeaways and exercises

Preparing for an interview can be a stressful occasion. We therefore recommend keeping a checklist prepared to ease some of that stress.

The checklist below summarizes what's been discussed in this chapter and serves to summarize the key points:

1. Review job description
2. Review company details
3. Determine industry
4. Know flagship product
5. Find latest company news and awards
6. Research company's geographic locations
7. Know company size (number of employees)
8. Recall your stories relevant to the job description
9. Review knowledge pool for interview questions
10. Tweak answer for "Tell me about yourself" question
11. Prepare final questions
12. Review salary range
13. Keep sample work on hand (if applicable)
14. Print copies of resumé and references
15. Ensure clothes are cleaned and ironed
16. Use Google Maps for location; check the routes and timing
17. Get a good night's sleep

You're all set to go!

Tomorrow is the big day. If you've gone through the seven steps outlined in this chapter, you're as ready as you'll ever be. That job is going to be yours!

CHAPTER 9

THE HOT SEAT

The big day has arrived and the curtain opens on the interview. It's now time to present your resumé-self in full-scale reality—nerves and jitters notwithstanding. Take solace in the fact that you're as prepared as you can ever be for this interview. Remember, it's not just your expertise that's being evaluated here. The company's representatives now want to see first hand the kind of person you are and whether you will be a cultural fit with the team and the company.

At this point, your attitude matters most of all and it will decide the outcome of this interview. *Ask not what your company can do for you but what can you do for your company.* Maintain this attitude and you're on the right track to your next job. What the company can do for you comes *after* the job offer.

Remember, even if you *don't* get hired, you gain valuable experience by preparing for and going through the interview. This will also be a learning opportunity for the next time. No matter what the outcome, remember that there will always be lessons learned. Stay positive.

Your arrival

By now, you've determined how long it takes to get to the location. Thanks to Google Maps and GPS technology, it's usually impossible to get lost. Still, remember to use Google Maps to factor in the time it suggests, whether you're travelling by car, Uber, cab or public transport. Also, if you're taking your own car, add some extra time to find parking—especially if you're headed to a busy and possibly unfamiliar downtown area.

Arrive 15 to 20 minutes early, but don't walk through the door just yet. You probably realize that arriving late is total no-no. *Don't be surprised if you don't even get interviewed if you come in late.* However, arriving too early is not a good approach either. When you walk into the reception area and say that you have an interview, the interviewer will be phoned immediately. We hate it when we've scheduled an interview for 11 a.m., and security calls at 10:30 to say that the person has arrived and is waiting downstairs. We certainly cannot meet with the candidate *now*, because we've scheduled a meeting for 10:30 a.m. Now there's an annoying distraction in our heads—the knowledge that the person is already there waiting.

After you've touched down at the location, don't announce your arrival at reception just yet. Wait five to 10 minutes before your scheduled interview time. In a smaller company, five minutes will be enough time for the interviewer to wrap up whatever he or she is doing, then head to the reception area to fetch you. (In a company that is spread across a wider space and with several buildings, 10 minutes might be preferable warning.)

So, what will you do for the time you have to kill from your arrival to the moment you present yourself to the reception or security desk? You'll be getting your game face on! Head to the washroom and settle any bio needs in there. You don't want a full bladder distracting you during the interview. Look at yourself in the mirror and calm your nerves. Rehearse some of the answers you've prepared in your head—*out loud* if you're *alone* in the bathroom.

There is a fantastic Ted Talk on body language by Amy Cuddy who demonstrates the effectiveness of *power poses*. We use these power poses before any stressful situations—the Wonder Woman pose is John's preference. We hope these power poses will also help you to overcome your nervous habits.

Exercise:

Head over to YouTube and search for "Ted Talk Amy Cuddy Body Language" to take 21 minutes out of your day to learn about her findings.

After you've announced your arrival at the front desk, you'll be waiting a couple of minutes for your interviewer to arrive. If it's a high security building, you will most likely be waiting on the ground floor lobby outside a security desk. In many cases, you will have arrived at the main office itself and will wait in the reception area. Be seated and look relaxed. If you notice a magazine or brochure about the company, pick it up and give it a read. This is a positive first sight of you from the interviewer's point of view.

Your interviewer will eventually arrive, and the interview begins!

Body language

Your body language is communicating throughout the interview—from the moment you enter the building until you finally step outside. Mind your posture when sitting both in the waiting room and at the interview table. Remember, this isn't the classroom where you can slouch back or lean on an armrest. People who mean business are *alert and upright*.

During the interview, arm-folding and leg-crossing are strictly not advised, as these actions suggest that you are closed to discussion or have something to hide. The biggest challenge some folks have is with hand gestures. These individuals can range from either appearing too reserved, by keeping their hands stuck permanently at their sides, to frantic, by flailing their hands all over the place—creating such a distraction that the interviewer is no longer listening to what is being said, and is instead battling the turbulence in the room caused by the arm movements! The mid-region is where your hands should be—on a short leash.

Be extra conscious of any distracting habits you may have. Nail-biting, leg-twitching, knuckle-cracking—keep it all bottled in until you've left the building.

> Connel has had an embarrassing hair-twirling habit since he was a child. In his adulthood, he has intentionally cut his hair very short before interviews to prevent this from happening, because he knows he won't be able to fight the urge. Considering his daughter has it too, his defense is that it's genetic!
>
> John believed that Connel was just particularly well-groomed during his interview—now he knows the truth!

Finally, remove all distractions—your smartwatch, Fitbit, cellphone and anything else that could beep, buzz, jingle and distract your attention. Looking at your watch *even once* during the interview could be a deal breaker! Some of us instinctively check our devices, even if we are not bored; the interviewer will not see it that way. It is a *requirement* that you completely silence your cellphone—powering it down is even better. You don't want to have to excuse yourself because your cellphone goes off. Your incoming calls will be directed to your voicemail. It's possible that you could be receiving a call for *another* interview (see chapter 5), so make sure that your voicemail is set up to make you sound professional (discussed in chapter 4).

Greeting and handshake

I don't need to learn how to greet people, I do it all the time. You may be tempted to skip over this part but you'd be surprised to know that one out of five people we meet for an interview tends to botch up the greeting in some way. It could be nerves or it could be just the kind of person you are. If you're extremely shy, you may not be confident about meeting people for the first time.

But the harsh truth is, regardless of your personality or jitters, there are standard rules when it comes to the greeting—no exceptions. Here they are:

1. Smile and be enthusiastic. You're *happy* to be there and *appreciate* the time and opportunity this person has given you. (But don't go overboard with enthusiasm. You don't have the job just yet!)
2. The handshake is the most common mistake. Keep these points in mind: If your handshake gives the other person the holding-a-dead-fish feeling, you've got to work out those forearms and tighten that grip. To some of the jocks: it's not a bone crushing contest.
3. Look the person in the eye during the handshake. This is another fairly common mistake we observe. The candidate offers up a superb smile and the perfect handshake… while looking at our shoes instead of our faces.

It takes all but a few seconds for any person, in this case the interviewer, to formulate a first impression of you. This is why your outfit and the greeting play an important role. When we meet somebody for the first time, based on his or her appearance, dress sense and the initial small talk on the way to the interview room ("How was your day?", "Did you find the place easily?") we know in 30 seconds how this interview will most likely unfold. Although we, as interviewers, try to fend off the biases and assumptions, they start to creep into our minds from the moment we greet the candidate. We are sure that any honest interviewer would admit the same.

Arriving at the interview room

You may be greeted by a few more people. These days, it's rare to be interviewed by just one person. Apply the same greeting rules as before.

Pay extra attention to names! It's possible that the person who initially meets you is the recruiter who was in contact with you, and then leads you to the hiring manager's office. When you hear names, pay close attention to them and reciprocate how they are referenced. If the recruiter says, "You're going to be meeting John. He's waiting in the board room," you can refer to John by his first name. If you're meeting someone higher up (say, a director or a VP), he may be referred to as "Mr. Ribeiro", in which case you follow the lead, and use Mr. Ribeiro. Based on the company's culture, these naming conventions may differ. In most organizations these days, however, people are on a first name basis. For the most part, the days of Mr. and Ms. are behind us. The backup strategy of course—if you've forgotten the name or it was just too hard to pronounce—is to use the simple Sir or Ma'am.

Pay close attention to the job titles of those in the room. One could be a manager and the other a director. The manager is generally more closely connected with the day-to-day tasks and operations of the department, whereas the director will have a high-level and strategic perspective. This could be helpful with directing your questions to the right person during the interview.

Your attitude

The most important part of the interview——*and we can't stress this enough*—is your attitude. Many candidates don't make the cut due to their attitude and demeanor during the interview. They say all the right things and are technically capable, but come off as too pushy, too reserved or overconfident. Once again, this is a good time to remind you of the purpose of this interview. It has nothing to do with *discovering* your qualifications or your experience. That was all covered in your resumé and obviously, it passed the employer's requirements or you wouldn't be here. You're at the interview for two reasons: to *validate* and *elaborate on* the experience from your resumé, and more importantly, to allow for an analysis of your *personality* and *cultural fit*.

Most managers know how an employee with a bad attitude or work ethic can be a constant thorn in their side, and firing a full-time employee is not an easy task in many organizations in Canada. First, there's the added expense of the rehire, and second, there may also be legal obligations to fulfil. For these reasons, hiring managers know all too well the consequences of a bad hire, and will analyze your personality thoroughly. Be aware and act accordingly.

We have highlighted some key personality traits to recognize. After going through them, reflect on yourself, and ask others how you match up in these areas. Your friends and family know your personality best, so seek their opinions if you are unsure.

Confidence

It's important to be confident. Your confidence will show in the quality and tone of your answers, your ability to look the interviewer(s) in the eye, your smile, lack of hesitation and direct responses. However, some candidates overstep their boundaries and come off as overconfident with an I-know-more-than-you-or-anybody-else attitude. Remember that the interviewer has just met you. You don't have an outstanding reputation (yet) that could allow you to be even remotely sarcastic or condescending about your abilities.

We had a candidate once who seemed to be an ideal fit for the role. She was bright, had a great personality, and even showed us case studies about her previous work and testimonials from her previous colleagues That was a first for us. This candidate really demonstrated that she could think outside the box and was innovative. Two thirds of the way into the conversation, however, the tide turned. When it became clear that we were impressed with her work, she let her own excitement get the better of her. She started making statements such as, "So once I'm part of your team, I will handle these problems and start this project for you, and you won't have to worry." Warnings went off in our heads: *Hold on! Slow down! You're not part of our team yet, and how do you know what problems we will have? This is a new department; even we don't know what problems we may have.* Toward the end, when we asked her if she had any questions for us, she replied, "No questions, I guess I'll just see you Monday." And the response in our heads was *Um, no you won't!*

This was an example of the perfect candidate who blew her chance. Her comments could have been more along the lines of: "Do you think your department would face these problems?" and "I hope you think I would be a good fit for the team with these skills." Instead, she just started assuming that we would need them. Her *overconfidence* lost her the job.

Earlier on in his career, John himself fell victim to overconfidence when he interviewed for a team lead role. When asked *"What type of animal would you like to be?"* he answered *"I would like to be a tiger, because tigers get whatever they want."* When they asked if he had any questions for them, he replied, *"Not really, I'm just eager to go on vacation right now and I'm dying to get out of here."* Talk about putting yourself in a "Don't call us, we'll call you" situation!

Experienced managers are also aware that overconfident individuals will not get along well with other team members. When they make mistakes, they will lie or BS their way to cover up the mistake, or even worse, blame somebody else. These individuals tend to have a my-way-or-the-highway attitude, even with their boss. Being employed doesn't mean that you always have to keep your mouth shut and do whatever your boss tells you to do, but there will be situations when you have to compromise for the sake of consensus of the team. Managers know this and will measure your level of confidence to see if you are willing to act on your skills and abilities, but not to a level where it compromises teamwork.

Honesty

If you don't know the answer, just say, "I don't know" or "I'm not 100 per cent sure of that." If you have a rough idea of what the answer might be, start with a disclosure statement: "I'm not a 100 per cent sure, but I think it's…"

A friend of ours once went through a job interview in which he either responded "I don't know" or "I don't have experience in that" to 50 per cent of the questions. He left that interview completely sure that he would not get the job. In truth, how he had even managed to get the interview was a mystery, so to his surprise (and ours), he was called back for a second interview. He was told: "Although you don't have the experience we were hoping for, we appreciated your brutal honesty. And you seem like a smart guy. I'm sure you'll learn the ropes with us." This friend is now in his 15th year with that company.

Dishonesty presents itself when you take credit for somebody else's work. Remember our STAR methodology for answering interview questions? If you're giving an example of a major accomplishment or details on a project, the manager will ask you to elaborate on your specific involvement. If you're claiming ownership of someone else's work, chances are you will be caught in the lie. You cannot know the intricate details of a job unless you've done it yourself.

As far as personality is concerned, honesty is one area where most people fail. And those who are exceptionally honest make the shortlist. It may not necessarily mean that we catch you in a lie (but if that happens, you might as well just walk out the room). Honesty is demonstrated through the *quality* of your answers. Quality means that the answer to the question is given immediately, and is direct and to the point. (Here's where the prep work pays off.) We once had a candidate who provided five-minute monologues for every question that we asked. We couldn't even complete the interview because we were already out of time halfway through the questions. At the end of each answer, we were so confused by the response that we weren't even sure whether he had actually answered the question.

In the end, if you've done all the prep work from the previous chapters, there should be little reason for you to be caught off guard and resort to dishonesty. You already have answers for the toughest questions—just be sure those answers speak the truth.

Humility

Confidence and honesty can be encompassed with the overlaying trait of humility. Humility can be felt when you arrive in the room, and it exudes from everything about you—your smile, dress sense, tone of voice and dialogue. Now we're not saying you have to be a saint, but employers do appreciate candidates who show some restraint in their mannerisms when answering or asking questions and in their overall demeanor.

A candidate with humility respects the interviewer as a representative of the employer. As such, this candidate doesn't speak out of turn or interrupt the interviewer. A candidate with humility chooses to make suggestions and requests, rather than to 'tell it like it is' or 'should be'. This candidate would never have a this-job's-already-mine attitude, or act as though he or she is doing the interviewer a favour by being there.

We once had a candidate who was given the wrong information by the administration team. He arrived at the building across the street from our own office (which also belonged to our company). He prattled on and on about how he was given the runaround by security and how much of his time was wasted. That interview was over before it even started! Being positive is also an expression of humility. Avoid negativity in any form. Don't complain about the commute, the weather or your old boss or company.

Be respectful of the hiring manager's time as well, even if that manager is not respectful of yours. Remember, the hiring process is not a fun activity for most managers because it has caused them to break their day-to-day routine. This constricts the time left in their schedule for their normal responsibilities.

Sincerity

Not to be confused with honesty, which is about being truthful, sincerity is about your motives and genuine consideration for a person's needs. It's possible to be honest but not sincere. For example, you can tell me of your interest in working in a particular industry because you would find it challenging and fulfilling. That's an honest answer because it's true. However, if you spend the rest of the interview complaining about past experiences and events when things always went wrong and declare that you don't see eye to eye with that industry's best practices, we would question your sincerity. If all you do is moan about the industry, it doesn't seem like you're genuinely motivated to be a part of it.

When it comes to the interview, your motives should be clear. This clarity will come from your answers to questions as well as the questions you ask. Considering the interviewer's needs, your motives should be:

1. I'm here to solve problems you have.
2. I want to be a part of this organization.
3. I want to learn and develop myself to fit your needs.
4. I want to get along with others in the team.
5. I'm willing to fill any gaps between my skills and experience and this job's requirements.

You may have other motives as well, but don't bring these up:

1. I need more money. **X**
2. I'm trying to get out of my old job because it sucks and may manager's an ass. **X**
3. You need to take care of me. When are we going to talk benefits? **X**

When preparing answers to your interview questions, keep sincerity in mind. Ultimately, the job offer will go to the person who demonstrates that he or she *can do* the job, *wants to do* the job, *wishes to be a part* of the company and *gets along* with others.

Respect

Remember who you're dealing with here. This is a professional stranger who has the authority to hire you and substantially change your life. As such, hiring managers deserve (and certainly demand) respect from you. They are your employers first, and not your friends. Respect their time (by being on time), and address them by Mr. or Miss depending on the culture of the organization you see and hear around you. If they are Gen X, they most certainly expect a certain level of respect and formality during the interview. "Whasssuuuup?" as your greeting is not going to win you any points with them. Save the informality until after you have the job and have established a relationship with them.

Ask intelligent questions

You will be presented with opportunities to ask questions during the course of the interview. You don't have to wait until the end for the manager to ask you if you have any questions.

The questions you ask will depend on how well you pay attention to the discussion. In the initial part of the interview, the manager will exclusively direct the conversation based on his or her questions. You will be asked about yourself and your experience. At some point, the manager will start talking about the company and the position that you're applying for. This is where your focus and attention goes into overdrive. *Hang on every word* this interviewer says and listen for clues as to where the focus and attention are being applied. Simultaneously, tap into your knowledge and expertise and ask questions during the manager's explanation *when appropriate*. This is not an invitation to interrupt. Wait for the point to be finished before you humbly ask, "May I ask a question regarding that?"

With preparation, you can formulate a smart problem-solving question in advance. Here is an example:

Manager	"In our call centre, management frequently requests performance reports, and my team is held accountable for the numbers that come out of those reports."
You	"Sorry to interrupt, but can I ask you a question about that? Because it's quite interesting."
Manager	"Sure."
You	"What exactly is measured in these reports? Is it average handle time and first-call resolution rates?" (That question comes from your experience.)
Manager	"Good question. You are right, it is AHT and FCR, but we also measure customer satisfaction rates and contact volume."
You	"Sounds similar to what my management was measuring as well. Judging by the size of the organization, I estimate that you probably anticipate a call volume of about 1,000 every month. Is that close?" (That comes from your homework on the organization's size.)
Manager	"It's going to be more like 1,500 per month during peak times."
You	"I had experience managing a project to reduce call volume. Maybe we can discuss that later—if you like and if there's time." (Note the attention you are bringing to your experience, coupled with the humility of asking for permission to speak to it—rather than just telling the manager about it—and your respect for the manager's time.)

The interview should, for the most part, be a two-way conversation. When you ask intelligent questions, the interview becomes a conversation rather than a turn-by-turn monologue. Through conversation, you each develop an understanding of the other person's character. This is not only important for the manager but for you as well. You need to know what you're getting yourself into. After all, you may be dealing with this manager 40 hours a week.

As mentioned in the previous chapter, the interview will start to conclude with the manager asking you if you have any questions. And the wrong answer is "No." Always ask the questions you have prepared for, and if you've uncovered new information during the interview, don't be afraid to revise them as needed. To continue from the example above, instead of asking, "What challenges would the call centre face?" you can personalize by saying "Since you mentioned Zero2Hired is opening a new branch in Toronto, would that have any impact on our team?" Another example could be "Since you've mentioned performance reports are important to the management, are there any initiatives ongoing or coming up to improve these numbers?"

The line between enthusiasm and desperation

Be enthusiastic about both the field and the job you're applying for. Your enthusiasm shines when you ask intelligent questions, speak with positive energy, talk about any communities, chapters or relevant organizations that you are part of, and share your past experiences and projects. You'll be given opportunities to speak to these points during the course of the interview.

But when you cross the line into desperation, that's when your enthusiasm starts to lose its charm with the interviewer. The I'll-do-anything-for-this-job attitude is a major detractor. If you start blurting out remarks along the lines of "I really need the money" or "I've been jobless for so long, I'll do anything you need me to do", the interviewer will start doubting your interest in developing your skills or your level of motivation once you're in. It's *never* good to appear desperate for work.

Good managers aren't looking for people who will clock in and do a minimal effort to earn a wage and leave. They want to hire people *better* than they are, people who will fill the gaps in the department and become resources to improve the efficiency of its operations by going above and beyond the job requirements. Although grateful to find a job, the previously desperate person will most likely not be one of these people. By contrast, the applicant who is enthusiastic about the job and his or her field of expertise will certainly be a much-needed problem solver in the department.

Remember, if you're desperate, that means you've been looking for work for a long time and have not found it yet. Maybe there's a reason why no one else will hire you. So, why should we?

On this subject, earlier we mentioned the importance of taking your sample work (if you have permission to show it) to the interview. Please avoid trying to make your sample work the main focus of the interview—it's not just your work that is under the microscope here, but your *attitude* and *personality* as well. Even if you have sample work that can bedazzle the world, don't be desperate to push it in their faces during your introduction. Wait for the opportune moment, then ask for permission to demonstrate your work (humility!) "Yes, I do have experience in this area. I've learned and developed so much with PowerPoint, including formatting digital financial reports for my boss. I have a sample of my work to show you—if you think it's relevant and would like to take a look."

Speak up

This section is for all introverts! The interview is not ideal for the silent types. Although introverts make up a good proportion (about half) of our society, some managers prefer recruiting people who are not reserved about speaking up and expressing their opinions and ideas.

> During one of Connel's interviews, the manager explained how his company's culture *required* that people speak their minds. This manager then ran Connel through a simulation in which he pretended to ask Connel to do something that he was not comfortable with. This simulation was developed to help the manager to judge how Connel would challenge his instruction.

Now we're not saying that being an introvert is a bad thing. In fact, of the two authors of this book, one is an introvert and the other is an extrovert. We'll let you decide who's who! Introverts won't speak up immediately. They need time to digest information (preferably alone), maybe do some research, and then make an informed decision and speak up. In this sense, some people say that introverts are more creative than their counterparts.

However, while you're on the hot seat, there's no turning back to think things through and do any research. You must ask questions and speak with confidence. The preparation work you did about the company and the position you're applying for should arm you with enough answers for the questions to be asked during that crucial hour. We also have another suggestion: You can prepare small-talk topics that you can feel comfortable speaking about after the initial greeting—sports, weather, community news, take your pick. With preparation, you can be an extrovert for an hour!

Wrapping up

When the interviewer asks, "Do you have any questions for me?" that's usually a signal that the interview is coming to a close. We've already discussed how to ask intelligent questions and how you've already prepared for this final round of questioning. Once your questions have been answered, the interview draws to a close. The final question you should ask is "So what's next in the interview process?" It's important to learn their plan for the interview process so you know what to expect. This question also shows that you're eager to move closer to the job offer.

The next step could be anything from "We will call you if you're chosen to start Monday" to "Now you are going to meet *Ms. Manager* from another department." Companies have different processes for conducting interviews. Sometimes it varies with the level of the position you're applying for.

State your appreciation for the interviewer's time with the same handshake you've practised before. You may be faced with a situation where the manager seems to be anxious to start his next interview on time. Most likely, these interviews are scheduled back-to-back and this manager knows all too well how delaying one interview will delay the rest of them. This is another opportunity to demonstrate professionalism and concern. Explain that you understand about the tight schedule with back-to-back interviews so you don't want to take up too much of anyone's time. Ask if it's okay to email any further questions you may have. Be sure to ask the manager for his or her business card, because you will need that contact information for the follow-up email.

You will follow the HR representative or maybe even the interviewer to the door or to next phase of the interview.

Tests

It's possible that you will be asked to complete online tests during the interview. These would most likely be technical tests, aptitude tests or typing tests. Depending on the job, some companies incorporate these tests into their interview process.

By now, every Millennial can ace a typing test. We were born to text, right? Still, it wouldn't hurt to be prepared. A laptop (or desktop) keyboard isn't the same as thumbing letters on a smart phone. It would be wise to at least practise an online typing test prior to the interview, just in case it comes up. They may not tell you in advance what the interview process is going to be like, so it's best to be prepared.

http://www.typingtest.com provides a free one-minute sample test to try out. Connel's score on this was 66 word per minute. Give it a try now.

You can also Google "free aptitude test" and take your pick, just to get a feel for what these tests can be like.

Finally, free technical tests are not so easy to find online. Most likely, the company you're applying to is paying a subscription specifically to use a technical test for recruiting purposes. If you're applying for an IT job, you are likely to be put on an online system to answer the questions. Don't worry about these technical tests too much. If you're applying for the right job that you're confident in doing, you should be able to pass. Some companies don't bother going through this level of detail for a test. Technical questions are usually asked verbally during the interview.

Handling an unprofessional interviewer

Not all interviewers know how to conduct a proper interview. You might think that this could work in your favour, but it may also work against you. An interviewer who is going with their gut and has not bothered to research or develop their own skills in interviewing will most likely ask the wrong questions, or not give you the opportunity to express yourself in a way that would get you the job. They can do this by asking a lot of closed-ended questions with Yes or No answers.

If you feel that you're not being asked the questions that speak to your experience, turn the interview around and start asking that interviewer questions that could lead to openings where you can speak to your experience. For example, if the interviewer asks closed-ended questions such as, "Do you meet with your team regularly?" you could reply, "Yes, I do, and when we get together, we actually gain a lot of experience and develop a lot of knowledge during those meetings. May I share some of my expertise in that area?"

Takeaways and exercises

Congratulations! You can now breath a sigh of relief that the interview is over. You can unclench your fists! You may come away from the interview thinking *Oh man! Why did I say that? I should have said...* Don't beat yourself up. It happens to us all, and the interviewer is aware of it. If it happened to you, it probably happened to the other candidates as well.

If you followed everything that was discussed in the previous chapters prior to coming to this interview, you were as prepared as you could have been—and likely more prepared than the other candidates. This means that you left very little margin for mistakes.

Now that the interview is over, the follow-up questions to ask yourself are listed in the following exercise.

Exercise:

As you come out of your interview, ask yourself the following questions:

1. Did I answer the questions confidentially by being direct and sticking to the point? Did the interviewer seem satisfied with the answer or did he/she have to repeat the question?

2. Did I show sincerity? Did I show that I was there to be a problem solver, to get along with others in the team, and to keep handling the department's challenges as my primary motives for this job?

3. Was I humble by being appreciative of their time and for being chosen to be interviewed among the hundreds of other applicants? Did I *not* act like a smartass know-it-all, and did I request permission to discuss a skill or talent that could solve a problem that they may have?

4. Was I brutally honest? Did I say "I don't know" when I had to?

5. Did I show an interest in the job and the company? Did I ask intelligent questions that addressed the needs of the company and the challenges of the department above my own personal needs?

6. Was I enthusiastic? Did I take care not to cross the line to desperation?

7. Did I have the right body language? Did I remember not to cross my arms or flail them about, and did I keep a careful check on my habits?

8. Did I ace all the tests?

If you've answered **Yes** to all the above questions, you couldn't have done a better job. Now it's up to the interviewer(s) to make the smart decision to hire you. Remember, they're pondering over whether you will be a right cultural fit to the department and organization. We hope you've demonstrated that you are.

The Toastmasters club where John is a member drives its exclusivity primarily on whether you'd be a good cultural fit to the organization. They have rejected professionally certified speakers because the interviewers did not feel that those individuals would commit to the organization and the community. They observe you when you're *not* speaking—are you taking notes, are you interacting with others, are you socializing well and being positive about becoming a member?

You face a similar challenge when you step into that interview room. So remember, you may have all the right credentials on paper but if you neglect the above guidelines on attitude and personality, you won't get the job.

It's not over yet. There is still opportunity to sway the job offer in your favour, and we will cover this in the next chapter. We have also yet to cover the juicy part of your salary and benefits.

CHAPTER 10

THE POST-INTERVIEW PROCESS

The interview does not end when you leave the building. Once you're out of sight, there's a good chance that you will be out of mind, *even if you aced the interview.* Remember, an unskilled interviewer does *not* work in your favour. One classic trait of bad interviewers is not remembering who their best candidate was.

After you've completed your interview, a dozen people may follow. The impact of your interview will be eroded with each new candidate who is interviewed. It's not intentional, it's just human tendency. As always, you need to take control of the situation even after the interview is over. This chapter lays out the steps to do just that.

Then, of course, there is the management of the ultimate goal—the job offer. We will highlight the details you'd need to look for and mull over when considering the job offer. Especially when you have *two* offers in your hand, how will you select one over the other?

The thank-you note

Once the interview is over, the interviewers are quite likely to forget you in the vortex of candidates they're meeting. And this is precisely what you're trying to prevent with the thank-you note. Its second objective is to show the interviewer(s) that you really want the job and you are enthusiastic (but not *desperate* for it).

The thank-you note should be completed before the end of the day. Once an interview is complete, set a reminder at the end of the work day, say 4 p.m., to send a thank-you email to each of the people who interviewed you. You have their contact details on their business cards that were handed to you while you were wrapping up the interview. (See chapter 9 to review this.)

In the email, thank each person for his or her time, express your interest in the job, and give a touchpoint on any information that was newly uncovered in the interview. It may go something like this:

> *Dear Mr. Ribeiro. I wanted to thank you for the time you took earlier today to meet with me and consider me for this position. Zero2Hired seems to have a really good culture and vibe to it, and the position that you explained to me in detail aligns with my skills in project management and documentation. As you stated, you require someone who is familiar with HTML coding and graphic design, and my experience certainly meets these requirements.*
>
> *I hope to hear from you again and to become part of the Zero2Hired team.*
>
> *Best regards, Connel*

If you've taken the initiative to create an online resumé, this is a good opportunity to insert the link on the line below your name. That will help to jog the recipient's memory of who you are.

To this day, only a handful of applicants have ever sent us a thank-you note after an interview, so this is another low-hanging fruit for you grab… and stand out from the crowd.

The follow-up note

After two days have passed, you are anxious to hear back from these individuals. Don't be discouraged if you hear nothing. It's entirely possible that they are still interviewing other candidates, or have chosen one. Still, you never know. With the dozens of applicants who may have been shortlisted, they may just have plain forgotten about you. That's where the follow-up note comes in. Just like the thank-you note, the follow-up note acts as a reminder to the interviewer about who you are and what you bring to the table. It may sound something like this:

> Hi Mr. Ribeiro. I trust you've been keeping well and had a great week. I wanted to follow up on the interview I did with you on Monday. As discussed, there would have been an update by the end of this week. Please let me know if you have any information about my application. I'm confident that this role in web development would be the perfect opportunity for me to enhance Zero2Hired's web content with an intuitive design and reliable performance. I look forward to hearing from you.
>
> Best regards, Connel

Once again, here's an opportunity to insert the link to your online resume. This could add even more value here, as days have passed since the interview. By now, the interviewer definitely needs a solid reminder of who you are.

When to send the follow-up note would depend on what was discussed during the interview. In most interviews, the manager commits to a one-week time frame, in which case you can send the follow-up note on day 5 or 6. If the manager specified a two-week time frame, there's no harm in sending a follow-up note after week 1, and another one closer to the end of week 2.

And of course, let's not forget LinkedIn. Be sure to add the recruiters to your LinkedIn network—so they can remember who you are in the short term and you can connect with them in the future as well.

Now that you've read and worked your way through the steps outlined above, it's time to stop and congratulate yourself for doing everything you could to position yourself for a job offer. While you wait, let's take a breath and turn our attention to the fascinating—and entirely necessary—topic of salary, benefits… and your expectations.

Salary and benefits

Here we are finally at the juicy part—the fruits of your labour! You should already have prepared a salary range that would be acceptable for you and for this role. Your salary expectations may already be known to the interviewer—if it was discussed during the pre-screening phone call with the HR recruiter or during the first interview. If the interview process contains a second interview and you're called back for this, you will likely negotiate your final salary at that interview.

We want to reiterate the importance of not undervaluing yourself for a lower pay in the hope of increasing your chances of getting the job. Remember that this position has a budget range, and as long as all candidates are within that range, it doesn't matter who asked for the lowest. The person who is the best fit for the job gets it, regardless of whether she asked for more than the other candidate. The budget for this position is not something you would know in advance. You can only assume that it's in the range of the market value, which we explained how to research in chapter 8.

When asked for your salary expectations, we like to hear something that sounds like this: "Well, I'm sure a company like … (*the company you are in discussions with*) would make a fair offer, and I'm happy accepting the current market value for this position. So, what is the budget range for this position?"

You may get a response that the budget range is between $45K and $50K, or that the budget for this position is $48K. You can respond, "Based on the research I have done, I was hoping for $52K. Is there any possibility that my skills and experience would allow for it?"

The conversation would continue from there. You must use your best judgment to know when to call it quits and agree on a figure. Don't argue for 10 minutes over it. You already know from your research what the market value is, and if the offer is within that range, it's fair.

Once the base salary has been agreed upon, you have a job offer. Congratulations! Your job track for this application has ended with an offer. But hold on—you're not done with the negotiations just yet. When a job offer is extended to you, it's usually in the form of a written or electronic document that contains all the other benefits you earn as a full-time employee with that company. Some contract positions may not be offered these additional benefits.

If, up to now, you have been unemployed, you most likely won't negotiate much on the other benefits. If you're switching jobs, however, you'll need to compare the benefits to those currently offered by your existing company. Every benefit has a value, and you don't want to lower your pay and lifestyle with your new company unless you really want to get out of your existing company. If company A pays you $60K per year with three weeks of vacation, you're being paid to work for 49 weeks a year, which amounts to $1,225 per week. If company B pays you $61K per year with two weeks of vacation, you're essentially being paid to work 50 weeks a year, which amounts to $1,220 per week. So, even though company B pays you $1K more, by receiving less vacation time, you are actually earning less per week.

The range of benefits offered to employees will depend on the size of the company (with the larger companies typically having a far wider range available). These are some benefits that might be on the table:

1. Bonus structure: Many companies have annual bonuses that depend on the employee's performance and the company's performance. Other factors could also influence the amount. This is direct money in the bank, and if your new company does not have a bonus plan, it's something definitely worth considering in the negotiations.

2. Medical insurance: Most large companies offer to provide a subsidized private medical insurance plan to supplement government health insurance plans. This is also an expense that would come out of your pocket and affect your bottom line, so it's worth looking into.

3. Wealth accumulation plans: Larger enterprise companies also offer group savings plans by tying up with financial investment companies. They may also have an opportunity for you to invest in their shares if it's a publicly traded company. They may also have a private pension plan in which they would match your contributions. All of this adds up to money in the bank, so it's important to consider.

4. Employee discounts: Again with large enterprise companies, you can benefit from discounted prices on certain products and services thanks to a pre-defined agreement they have with their corporate partners in the discount program. Plus, you can

certainly benefit from employee discounts on your new employer's products and services if you use them. If you join an airline, for example, expect to enjoy generously subsidized airfare tickets to its destinations.

Don't forget to consider your commuting expenses as well. For example, if your new company pays you $2,000 more per year than your existing company—but is based in the downtown of a major city—you may actually be losing money because it may cost you $3,000 per year to commute from the town where you currently live.

Once the job offer is with you, the ball is in your court. At this point, you will almost exclusively be dealing with the HR recruiter on salary and benefit negotiations, as this would be in the HR realm. The recruiter may discuss any changes to the original job offer with the hiring manager for approval. Ultimately, any costs to the company for hiring will come out of the hiring manager's budget.

Handling rejection

Rejection is part of the game. We're sure that many of you have experienced it in some shape or form. Many people fear rejection, and we can certainly relate. Keep reminding yourself that every rejection is a learning opportunity in the hiring process. If, after your follow-up communication, you hear that the hiring manager has chosen someone else, take the initiative to email back one more time so you can understand why you were declined the job offer. It will definitely be valuable information. It may sound something like this:

I'm sorry to hear that, Mr. Ribeiro. If you don't mind, I'd like to hear your feedback on the interview I had with you. I'd appreciate an honest answer as I'm eager to learn how I can improve myself for the next interview I face.

The feedback you receive most certainly will be useful to you. It may even be something that you were completely oblivious to, and that's exactly the kind of information that you want to gather. It will improve your self-awareness and increase your chances of nailing the next opportunity. And here is the other place where the job track can end for this application.

Keep the momentum going

It's important not to lose focus on other jobs tracks. Don't think to yourself, *I've nailed that interview, *phew*. Time to kick back and wait for the offer to come in.* As we've seen in the previous section, rejection is possible, so don't let overconfidence and false hopes cause your other job tracks to suffer. Stick with the process, and dedicate the same hours to your job search as you did before this interview. Believe us, you will end up landing multiple job offers, which will further empower you during negotiations.

Conclusion

And so, we hope you're now better equipped with the right knowledge and understanding for tackling the rigours of the job hunt. It's definitely a competitive sport in the professional arena, but you don't have to be the fastest or the strongest to win—just the most prepared.

We hope you've discovered that it's all about being unique and standing out of the crowd, by getting personal and reaching out directly to the people who are empowered to hire you—or to contacts who can help you reach those people. This process positions your resumé so that it will be opened, which is half the battle! Then, it's all about sharpening your interview skills and being ever vigilant of the dos and don'ts during the interview.

Above all, it's realizing that the job hunt process is a job on its own. Dedicating several hours per day for five days a week is entirely possible, but the more dedicated you are, the shorter your days of being out of work will be. It certainly takes will and determination to do this, especially in today's world where temptation and distraction surrounds us at every turn—the alluring buzz or warble of a new social media message arriving on your smartphone, the latest episodes of *Game of Thrones*, or the gang getting together for brunch. If you had a real job, you wouldn't skip work to engage these indulgences. Your job hunt should be no different.

With that, our next congratulatory chapter gives you some general career advice to help you sail through your first 90 days on the job.

CHAPTER 11

YOUR CAREER, YOUR FUTURE

And so begins a new chapter in your life, at a place where you will be dedicating 40 to 50 hours each week, forging new relationships, learning new skills, developing yourself personally and, oh yeah, making money! Protect your career and nurture it by honing your talents, seeking and capitalizing on opportunities, and showing your boss that you're a solution provider.

But first things first—it's your initial 90 days. Your priority is to get your feet on the ground and build a strong foundation. If this is your first job, setting off on the right foot will allow you to progress up the ladder more quickly. Of course, if this is not your first rodeo, it's a chance to start with a fresh, clean slate.

A word of caution: In your first couple of months (maybe up to six) you will be on a probationary period with the company. This is essentially a stage in which the company is testing the waters with you to see if you're a good fit with the organization and the team. This is normally mentioned on the job offer or employment contract. During this time, the company can let you go without any legal obligations. It may seem harsh, but this is the norm in most companies. Don't take it as a warning. As long as you do your job well, you have nothing to worry about. It's just worth mentioning, however, that you need to be on high alert during this probation period.

Overall, just remember that even though you maybe confident in your skills and abilities, in the early days, nobody on the team knows who you are or what you're capable of. They will be skeptical about you until enough time passes and you've proven yourself to the team. This is actually a good thing, because you now are in control of how people perceive you in the organization, and you have a clean slate objective to foster a positive perception of yourself and your brand.

The first 30 days

Culture

The company's culture encompasses everything from the way people dress to the way projects are managed, so it's important to understand and adapt to the culture. How this culture developed, not many really know for sure.

We do know that the senior leadership of a company has a stake in influencing the culture. How that group chooses to run the business based on its collective skills and expertise normally remains fairly consistent. Over time, this results in patterns and observations that intermingle and create the corporate culture. For example, if the Chief Information Officer (CIO) of the company has a background in finance, it would be expected that results of the IT department (a direct report) would be depicted in numbers, with pie charts and graphs. (We all know that finance folks love to play with numbers.) This need would be asked of the CIO's subordinates and of their subordinates and so on. Thus, a culture of working with numbers and creating charts and reports during meetings would emerge within the IT departments of the company.

Here are some other examples of culture:

Dress Code: Probably the first noticeable aspect of culture. On your first week, you'll want to play it safe and come to work in more standard business attire—with a tie (men), or even a suit (women and men). These days, a lot of North American companies are adopting casual attire to work. Ask your manager about the dress code to get solid confirmation on it before you start wearing flip flops and skate shorts to the office.

Meetings: Understand how meetings are conducted in the organization. Some companies may be strict with timing; others allow five to 10 minutes of slack before the meeting begins. Understand how meetings are created using the technology and facilities available. Get a feel for how meetings progress as well. Do the organizers keep it short and sweet? Do the participants joke around during the meeting or is it all business? Does management insist on agendas prior to organizing meetings? (This is a good habit that some cultures have adopted.)

Collaboration: This is an important buzzword that's currently popular among large corporations. It describes how departments coordinate and work with one another toward a common goal. Large enterprises usually struggle with collaboration because of their sheer size. It's challenging to know who does what on other teams. On the other hand, companies with transparent cultures that practise synergy between teams usually make sure that any endeavour or new goal always keeps other stakeholders in mind.

Communication: What is the primary means of communication in the company? Email, of course, but chat is also becoming popular in some organizations. Are there traditional landline phones or has the company moved on to VOIP? How do people communicate with customers or staff from overseas?

Technology: Are most people given laptops or desktops to work with? If laptops are a default, are you expected to work from home? How do you connect to your IT services in and out of the office network? What technology is used for the management of documents and other information? Is paper frowned upon and are you expected to keep your documents digital most of the time?

Security: What are the policies surrounding security of information and physical access to the office? Speaking of policies, what other standard policies are in place when dealing with staff, customers or vendors? This information may be covered during your company orientation with HR, or your boss may have the task of ensuring that you're aware of these policies.

Conversation: How do people speak to each other? Is it all business all of the time? Are there moments when you can joke around? Do people jokingly swear at each other or is that frowned upon?

As we discussed in chapter 3, **http://www.glassdoor.com** provides a highly informative way to investigate aspects of corporate culture from anonymous comments and ratings of employees. It will give you an idea of what the culture is like. Just remember not to be too swayed by the odd negative comments of a disgruntled employee.

Get to know your team

Unless you're working in a lighthouse or at the North Pole, you are most certainly going to be part of a team. As such, you have to make sure that you get along with your team members. It's one of the qualities that your manager liked about you when you were hired, so don't disappoint.

The first team member you'll need to know best is… your manager, of course! He or she is the person you will likely be working closely with most of your time, and it's within this person's authority to reward you with opportunities when they arise. Of course, established Millennials know first hand that not every boss is the ideal manager. Every person is different and every manager has his or her own unique style to management and leadership. Some managers are natural leaders or have taken the initiative to learn to be good leaders. Others, not so much. Now, we wouldn't go so far as to say they'd be like Kevin Spacey in *Horrible Bosses,* but don't expect your boss to be your buddy, mentor or coach. Many managers are too wrapped up in their own work to initiate those conversations that start with, "So how're you doing?" Still, this could work in your favour if you play your cards right. Managers who are wrapped up in their work will gladly welcome any opportunity or plans that relieve them of their stress and workload, and this is where you could swoop in with those ideas. This is what you were hired for, remember? To be a problem solver. So as far as getting to know your boss is concerned, try to figure out that person's pain points in the routine work and see if you can lend an extra helping hand. We say "extra" because most likely you will be solving a couple of problems for your manager by default because that's what your position is designed to do.

It would also be helpful to know other factors such as: How does the boss prefer to communicate? Email or face-to-face? Observe that person's emotions and ways of dealing with stress. When does your boss like to be left alone? What's that person's tolerance to interruption when you have a question? Does the boss like to joke around or is it all business? Are you given the freedom to make your own choices or does the boss micromanage? How available is he or she—is there an open door or do you have to schedule every conversation? How does this person expect you to report results of your work—formalized reports via email or verbal updates? And finally, how open is your boss to change and suggestions? Don't expect everyone to accept change with open arms.

And then there is the rest of the team—the people you will be working with who may or may not report to the same manager as you do. It's important to develop a rapport with these folks as well, because from the manager's perspective, the department's problems cannot be solved by one person. The accomplishment of the manager's goals can only happen with collaborative team effort.

Team members who do not get along present a major thorn in the manager's side. Don't contribute to that. In your personal life, there are likely folks you don't see eye to eye with, and yes, there is a possibility that you will have to deal with the same kind of person five days a week. Unlike in your personal life, you can't give a team member in your office you work closely with the cold shoulder. You also have no authority over whether this person stays or leaves. You must make an effort to cooperate with your team members, and that means understanding how each individual works and thinks, as well as gaining better knowledge of his or her character.

You could analyze the following traits about your team members:

1. Do they prefer to communicate via email or in person?
2. Are they strictly focused on business or is there room for humour and lighthearted banter?
3. How does everyone accesses common data?
4. Are team members reserved about discussing their work or do they share their efforts with the team?
5. Do they tend to work collaboratively or in silos?

Answers to these types of questions may be the same across the team, but individual team members will have their own unique personality.

Listen more than talk

As you develop relationships with team members and your manager and figure out the pain points of the department, you need to listen more than talk. You will be tempted to show them your stuff right off the bat, and by all means, if you are confident that it's something that will add value to the team, go for it. But be extra cautious in these early days. Remember, you are still making a first impression with the team. Any mistakes early in the game could brand you as a goof-up.

Listening to the team's heartbeat in the first month will help you to make an informed decision about the timing of your first initiative. Be sure that it's what the team needs to improve, rather than just flaunting your skills. Early in the game, talking too much about the strength of your skills and your past achievements may give the impression that you're a know-it-all.

Learn the technical ins and outs of your job

The better equipped you are with managing the technical aspects of your job, the more reliable you will be. The first 30 days will involve training, and someone, possibly your manager or a co-worker, will be teaching you the basics. The technical aspects could either be related to technology (such as learning a special software) or departmental processes.

Training may either be formalized in a classroom environment with a dedicated trainer or provided informally by a co-worker. Aim for a good rapport with the trainer—you will need this person's help and guidance along the learning curve. If this is informal training, it may be an inconvenience to the co-worker just as the interview process is a bother to the manager. That person is required to break away from an already busy schedule to cater to this ad hoc task. So, don't expect the co-worker to be thrilled about training you.

Try to grasp everything you can and *take notes!* You may be the type of person who thinks notes are for sissies, but we can assure you, this does not create a good impression. One of the first on-the-job details about you that will be analyzed is your ability to learn. If you're a slow learner, that will be spotted quickly. Making an effort to take notes will significantly reduce any slow learning gap that you may have.

You must master the technical aspects of your job ASAP, so that you can move on to better things down the road.

The first 60 days

Build positive relationships with co-workers

Once you've successfully passed the first lap, you've started to build trust with your team and maybe even zeroed in on team members with common interests with whom you can form positive relationships. Some team members may have been in the company for a while and have already experienced the stages you're going through right now. If you've formed a positive relationship with these folks, you can start to seek their advice on how the department functions, what they do best and where they feel that something is lacking. Perhaps you can understand more about the company's culture and structure through them.

Your knowledge of the organization will have considerable influence on your career with that company. Whenever a special task must be done, the person with more knowledge about the company will be able to identify key stakeholders who need to be involved and informed.

Understanding the organizations strengths and weaknesses

During your second month, you usually fall into a better routine. You should be starting to feel as though you're fitting in. At some point, you will start to recognize what the department does well and where there are gaps. Understanding where these weaknesses are could be a stepping stone for you toward proving your value to the team, *especially if their weakness is your strength.*

Connel once joined a new team that lacked organizational structure and procedure. With his strengths in process and documentation, he suggested creating a Policies and Procedures document for the department's operations. This definitely earned him brownie points with the management, as they also observed his initiative to fix something that was broken.

As you identify aspects of the company's culture through the actions of your manager and your team members, notice what they often complain about. Determine whether you can contribute in some way to resolving that problem but make sure that it's something you can confidently do. You don't want to fumble your first special task.

Provide positive feedback

Your manager will undoubtedly ask you, "So how's it been going so far?" *Stay clear away from complaints.* Don't give your manager any impression that you're unhappy, especially during your probation period! Be positive about the work environment, the people you work with and the organization's culture. The time for criticism will come *after* you've established yourself as a reliable resource.

Additionally, be selective when making references to your previous company. You can utilize skills from your past, but aspects of your previous organization's culture probably won't work with your new company. When you provide constructive feedback, make sure that it's coming as a suggestion from you and is justified because *you* think it's the right thing to do (not because that's the way your previous company did it). Some managers can be quite territorial about their department and company, and possess a we-do-things-differently-here mindset. Be sure to provide every suggestion from the standpoint of *your own observation and analysis of this team.*

Understand the department's goals

Without exception, every department has goals. These may include providing the best customer service experience, meeting sales targets, saving the company money or ensuring that customers' payments are received on time.

Your manager will definitely know what these goals are. When having that positive-feedback conversation with your manager, ask again what the department's goals are for this year. Yes, goals can change year on year, so it's essential to stay informed of the current priorities.

Ask your manager about the biggest challenges to meeting these goals. You will need this information later when you present your ideas to face these challenges.

Understand the company's core values and principles

The department's goals complement the company's overall guiding principles and values. These are usually listed on the company portal and website. Although the high-level principles and values are not discussed on a day-to-day basis, it's helpful to keep them in mind. They can provide a guide and reference when you are formulating an idea.

For example, if one of the values of the company is to always foster innovation, it can come up in a conversation that begins with: "Hey John, trying to be innovative here. Tell me what you think of this idea…"

The organization's core values are often overlooked, especially when the senior leadership teams do not take steps to reinforce the message. Employees tend to become focused on meeting their deadlines and getting through their daily operational tasks. They don't stop to reflect on whether their activities align with the company's values and beliefs. It's important to keep the core values in mind because your year-end performance review may be based on these values and beliefs in some way. You can also use them as an anchor to your initiatives in the future. If you're going to do something that is aligned with the company's values or beliefs, it will likely be endorsed—if resources are available.

The first 90 days

With the first 60 days complete, you've likely acquired a strong grasp of the basic mechanics of your job functionality. In addition, you now have an understanding of the company's and department's goals and objectives. You've also created positive relationships with your team members.

Find learning resources

Millennials are eager to develop themselves and progress through their career by acquiring new knowledge. Medium and large organizations normally have a learning and development program or educational resources that you can use for free. Ask your manager or HR business partner about these resources and if you can be involved in the programs. People of all generations consider the desire for and pursuit of learning to be a sign of taking your job seriously and wanting to improve. And if you can manage to apply what you've learned, you've taken your career to a higher level.

Find a mentor

Although you're now well into the flow of your work and are making progress, it's also a smart idea to find a mentor early in your career. Emerging Millennials will exponentially learn from experience—from both a technical and people perspective. For example, in the workplace, simply developing a great idea and wanting to implement it isn't enough. There is always some length of red tape that an employee has to work through to have that idea accepted and approved. Every manager for whom either of us has worked has been a mentor who's helped us to understand the organization's politics. We've learned something different from most but not all of our managers. Your mentor does not have to be your manager. Instead, a work colleague on the team, or even a manager from a neighbouring department could take this role.

Create your persona as a solution provider

There will be several personalities on your team. There's the person who complains a lot. There's the person who's the most cheerful. There's that guy who jokes around. There's that women who is super organized. What role will you take? You can be a combination of many personalities; some of them will come naturally from your own character. One personality that you want to be is the solution provider (a.k.a. problem solver). Remember that all jobs exist because there is a *problem* that needs to be anticipated or solved. Your manager and company leadership are constantly battling with problems that come their way, and anyone who can constructively find solutions to these problems will be appreciated. To do this, you must embrace change and always look to improve. No matter how well you think a process is running, there's always, *always* room for improvement.

Now that you're into your third month on the job, you will have noticed that certain things around you can improve. You may have a few or a multitude of ideas, but when communicating these ideas, take care to always keep the department's and company's goals in mind. For example, you know that the department is currently facing challenges collecting financial receivables on time from several customers. Suggesting a new software program with new and improved formatting to make your work easier that you found online is not the best idea right now. How will that make customers pay us faster? These customers are not complaining about the invoice formatting. A little investigation of the challenge reveals that some of the delay is caused by managers not available to sign checks during the summer time, as they are on vacation. So then, a good idea would be to shorten the customers' credit period just before the holiday months in August and December.

As Millennials, many of you would be bursting with ideas. But don't be disheartened if they don't receive approval. In the past and still today, many of our ideas have been rejected by management. But we never lose heart and keep the ideas flowing, always ensuring that our ideas are aligned with the department's and the company's goals and objectives. There are also other constraints to bear in mind. Maybe you have an idea that speaks directly to a goal or objective, but the biggest constraint is always lack of resources—time, money, or both. If the end of the financial year is approaching and the department's budget is almost depleted, the chance of acquiring that new software is slim. It's important to learn to take criticism and to continue turning those wheels in your head to come up with the next idea. Millennials have been labelled as whiners. Don't let that stick. Just take the hits and keep the ideas coming.

On that note, it's also vital to follow through your ideas with an action plan. If you think that your job is done by just coming up with the concept—and someone else can now do the grunt work of putting it into play—you will be sadly disappointed, and so will your management. Don't bring an idea to the table if you're not going to *own it* by formulating a plan to implement it.

Learn about the organization

If you work in a large enterprise, don't limit your knowledge to just what's going on around your department or division. Chances are, at some point you'll want to make a parallel move to another team. Your best bet to make that happen is learning about other departments and divisions too.

Keep in touch with what's happening with the customer-facing side of the business as well. This includes knowing about latest products, industry trends, the C-level executives' vision for the current year, and who the company's competitors are as well as their strengths and weaknesses. You'll never know when you meet a director from another department and impress that person with your knowledge of his or her involvement with the business.

To this day, we're surprised to see how uninformed people around the office are about their company. Granted, it's not possible to know everything that's going on in a large corporation. It's definitely a lot easier to have an overall knowledge of the business in a tightly knit start-up company. But large organizations usually have a corporate communications department that advertises the company's achievements and trends. Unfortunately, these broadcasts are generally ignored by most. People are so caught up in their own world that they rarely drop the blinders to see what's going on around them. Don't be that way. Keep the blinders on only when it matters. Take them off once in a while and expand your knowledge about the business. One day, that knowledge will come in handy for your next career move.

Your future with your career

Notice we said "your career" and not "your company". As we stated right at the beginning in chapter 1, true job security comes from relying on yourself and not on your company. Whichever company you're in, your priority should be to develop yourself both from a technical perspective and from a professional experience perspective. By "professional experience" we mean developing your teamwork skills by interacting positively with others, taking initiatives that support your current team's goals and objectives, and adjusting your personality (such as your speech mannerisms, your approach to tough situations, etc.) as you become more adapted to the culture. As you can see, you're not developing yourself selfishly—you keep the team and solutions to your department's problems a priority *and* develop yourself at the same time.

With our collective management experience and research, we'd like to conclude with some valuable advice that we hope will take root in your career. If you're an emerging Millennial, it's wise to take these points into consideration early so you succeed more quickly. Established Millennials may have already learned these lessons (the hard way?), but can perhaps learn something new here.

Be positive

Easier said that done? This advice is so simplistic, yet we continuously see members of the team walking around our department with a permanent cloud over their head. It's easy to be upset and disgruntled, and being positive takes effort—especially if you're in a team where the culture doesn't fit well with your personality.

Do you think you're a positive person? Being positive is more than just having a smile on your face. Reflect back on your past week. How many times have you complained about something each day? How many times have you vented your frustration at somebody else? How many times did you spread negative gossip and info about someone else? Ask yourself again if you were really as positive as you were the previous week.

If you truly want to have a positive outlook, you shouldn't be complaining about the work or the people in your department. You've been given a job to do and you must do it. You work with people who were *not* chosen by you, but you still have to figure out how to get along with them. If you are seriously unhappy with any aspect of your job, talk to your manager or the challenging person about it. Bottling it up will naturally result in negativity, and the cloud will start to grow above your head. If you let that cloud build up, it will start to fog your judgement and eventually effect your work performance.

Managers don't like having negative people on their team. People generally dislike having negative conversations, unless they are the perpetually pessimistic type. There have been some individuals in our work environments with whom we simply despised having conversations. Every time we saw them approaching, we would think, "Oh great, here he comes again. *Now* what?" Do you really want your manager thinking the same way about you? Ironically, opposites attract. I've observed that the negative people always find the positive people to vent their frustration on. If you're a positive person, good for you! When dealing with a negative personality, see it as a bonding opportunity and a chance for you to give positive advice and to strengthen your relationship.

Have constructive 'we' ideas

As we write this book, there are two members on our team who always have ideas. They frequently send emails with suggestions of new concepts and initiatives. But there is a stark difference between the two.

One person sends these types of statements:

> 1. "I would like to handle customer satisfaction projects."
> 2. "I want to switch to chatting with customers more often. I think I would be more productive."
> 3. "I think if I handle more calls, I can get my customer satisfaction scores up because I'm better on the phone"

The other person sends these types of statements:

> 1. "If we have our analysts take 10 minutes off the phone every day, they can take ownership of their customer interactions and follow up with them."

2. "I developed a little automation tool that has helped me re-duce the time taken to solve that software glitch problem in half. Can we roll this out to the team so that we can all use it?"
3. "Can I have write access to the knowledge base? Whenever I see the content is incorrect, I want to modify it so that others don't make mistakes."

Can you spot the difference? The first person has ideas, but they are all centred around themselves. We're not saying that's bad—after all, a person who is trying to develop him or herself is making a step forward.

The second person is trying to affect change that will help the *whole team* (we). And that represents several steps forward, because it also demonstrates leadership skills. Come performance review time, our brownie points go to the second person. Also worth mentioning here is that these ideas keep our department's objectives and goals in mind. We are striving to improve our customer service, aiming to shorten the time it takes to support customers, and trying to ensure that our documentation is accurate.

We mentioned this earlier on in the chapter, but it's worth mentioning again. As Millennials, we are hardwired to create positive change through our ideas and our initiative. Be constructive with your ideas by making sure that they align with your department's and company's goals and objectives. If improving employee morale is not on the goals list at the moment, don't suggest installing an Xbox in the break-out area just yet. And always make sure that *most* of your ideas are 'we' ideas that target the team and not just yourself. These ideas will have the most impact on your team and on your manager's positive perception of you.

Develop your emotional intelligence

Emotional intelligence has been a hot topic for a while, and lately has been picking up momentum as it applies to the workplace. The intelligence that you are born with is referred to as your IQ (based on an Intelligent Quotient test). However, your personal grasp on your own emotions, along with your understanding of the emotions of people around you, is referred to as your emotional intelligence and is measured by an EQ test. Fortunately, these important and useful skills can be learned and practised.

People with high EQs don't let emotions such as anger, excitement, guilt, fear or sadness cloud their judgement. With their clear judgement, they are able to make the right decisions regardless of their emotional state, but these people are not unfeeling robots. It has been said that courage is not being afraid, but from an EQ perspective, courage is actually the ability to do the right thing when you *are* afraid. People with high EQs are able to do the right thing regardless of their emotional state. They recognize the triggers that upset or excite them, they are aware of the physical changes to their body when an emotional situation presents itself to them, and through this recognition and awareness they are able to control their basic human urge to act on emotion, and then actively make the right decisions.

It's extremely important to continuously develop emotional intelligence in the workplace. The reality is that you will occassionaly become angry, frustrated, excited and guilty. And you will find yourself in the middle of a conversation or in the middle of making a decision while feeling these emotions. Making the wrong decision because of inadequate emotional intelligence could include:

1. Yelling at your co-worker in public because he didn't complete the task you were relying on to start your work on time

YOUR CAREER, YOUR FUTURE

2. Cutting off your boss in the middle of his presentation because you got excited about your knowledge about a point that
he was making

3. Feeling guilty about someone else's mistake even though it
was not your fault, and then overstepping your boundaries to
try to correct it—and your boss didn't appreciate that!

These are few examples of situations in which your emotions can get the
better of you and where your wrong decisions could have a lasting affect.
Although it's not easy to develop EQ, it's not impossible. A great
reference and book that we use as a guide *is Emotional Intelligence 2.0* by
Travis Bradberry and Jean Greaves.

It's a smart idea to learn to keep your emotions in check at all times.
Managing emotions is a deep and meaningful part of human
development that deserves a book of its own. We strongly suggest that
you research this topic on your own and work on containing your
emotions. You'll know that you've conquered your emotions when your
reactions are not based on impulse, but on *choice*.

Always take the high road

If you have your emotions in check, it will be a lot easier to take the high
road in those sticky situations where you have a disagreement with a
colleague. It's unavoidable—someone is going to piss you off, and the
last thing you want is to fly off the handle. Not only do you risk souring
the relationship, breaking a few HR rules and being labelled as someone
without control of their emotions (especially by your manager), but in
the worst case, unchecked emotions can lead to making bad decisions.

Taking the high road simply means making the right decision, even if it
means walking away from a conversation. We human beings are
designed to act *first* through our emotions, before the voice of reason

P a g e | 215

kicks in. This is how signals travel through our brain. Those who have a higher emotional intelligence are able to recognize this and use their decision-making to trump their emotions. Ergo, they take the high road. Once again, this is no easy task, and perhaps emerging Millennials will learn this through experience alone. We've all had those moments when we said to ourselves *Oh, why did I say that? I should have said this!* Develop your emotional intelligence and be aware that your emotions, if unchecked, can lead you to make bad decisions. Be on guard!

Manage your time

You listed time management as a skill on your resumé, right? Until today, it's rare that the two of us come across someone who manages his or her time effectively, taking the time to plan their day ahead of them and then sticking to that schedule. Time management does not mean multitasking (which is really doing several things at once under the misconception that you're getting a lot done). You may be occupied with a task, but you're doing a half-assed job if you're trying to juggle multiple things at once.

Take the time to read the amazing New York Times Bestseller on time management, *15 Secrets that Successful People Know about Time Management* by Kevin Kruze. Then you'll know what time management really is all about. We encourage you to research this topic along with emotional intelligence.

Time management is about understanding that *the only resource you can't get back is time*, and therefore prioritizing your work. As human beings, we have spells of motivation and productivity that we need to capitalize on, and not waste it on doing no-brainer work like email. It's also about understanding that every Yes to something is a No to something else. You have to make sure that you don't take on more than you can handle. Successful people in the world have this in common: their understanding of the value of time. If you take the effort to properly develop time management, you can accomplish much more for your team (and for yourself).

Communicate

In this section, we're not referring to the specifics of verbal and body language, which were covered during the interview in chapter 9. Instead, this section is about initiating a conversation between you and another person—yes, *actually communicating*.

Never underestimate the value of face-to-face or voice conversations. Texting technology including email, 'chat' and SMS has led people to succumb to disconnection from personal interactions with other people. As Millennials, we've grown up in a world where texting has become the norm for communication. But remember that nothing will ever outdo the impact of personal connection with people—either face-to-face conversations or voice conversations over the phone.

We work with a certain individual in our company who defies the company's culture by never responding to emails, and when he does, it's never more than two sentences. He's a senior manager and has obviously achieved great success in what he does, but the team has such a negative view of his work ethic simply because he prefers personal communication over email. He's a hard worker who gets the job done, but it's obvious to everyone that to spark any action from this person it is essential to have a personal conversation with him. Yet, people still avoid dealing with him directly as though talking to someone directly to accomplish a task is taboo.

If you want to move ahead in your career, get used to the habit of dealing with people at a personal level—face to face, voice to voice. Reserve text-based communication for its intended uses—mass communication, document sharing, quick clarifications or FYIs.

Foster positive relationships with co workers

You find a whole spectrum of personality types in the office environment, everyone from Jane who wants to be everyone's closest buddy to Jack who's all about the *work, work, work*. Recognize these personality types and deal with them accordingly. The workaholics may appear to be cold, blunt and to the point. It's nothing against you, so don't take it so hard. Some people have split personalities in the office—friendlier than a wet dog in personal conversations but as blunt as a hammer when it comes down to work.

You will be creating relationships with the people on your team and perhaps with those outside your team, depending on your position. Don't burn bridges with anyone. This will not be seen positively by your manager. If the person in question has a reputation for being difficult, your boss may understand why the relationship is going sour, but if you manage to foster a working relationship with this person at the very least, that will be all the more impressive.

Finally, never, never give in to the temptation of talking negatively about another person you work with in the office. As grandma said, "If you don't have anything nice to say, don't say anything at all." There is nothing to gain from speaking ill of co-workers, whether it's to their face or behind their back. State the facts of the situation and let people's own perceptions do the talking. This is the professional approach.

Be part of the solution, not the problem

Have you ever come across a personality type who complains a lot? All they do is whine and moan about what's wrong with their lives and situations. It's very hard for a complainer to be part of the solution. They may think they are by just highlighting a million problems, but that is *not* being part of the solution.

"Hey Connel, this is broken, so is that, and this needs fixing too. I can't work like this."

"OK, I hear what you're saying. Any ideas on how we can fix it?"

"That's not my job."

Sheesh

As stated earlier, every job exists to prevent or solve the problems within an organization. You and your manager need problem solvers and solution providers to get them through the many challenges their department inevitably faces. Not everyone is skilled or talented or motivated enough to be this person. The basic functions of your job solve certain problems, but new challenges will always appear. "Who amongst you will step up to battle this challenge?" thinks a manager about his team. If you can create the personality that brings your face to the manager's mind when there is a problem to be solved, that's the sweet spot where you'd like to be.

Again, we caution you on this front. Remember, it's imperative to solve problems with constructive 'we' ideas. And more importantly, don't bite off more than you can chew. Until you've been promoted to a new role, your manager still needs you to do the job that solves the problems you were originally hired for. If you come up with a solution to a problem, make sure you own it by seeing it through to the end. Don't just come up with the idea and assume it's going to be delegated to somebody else to move forward.

How do I get promoted?

We are asked this question a lot by our team—everyone wants to climb the corporate ladder and enjoy the recognition, the job title and the money that come along with it. When you work in an organization, there are three ways through which you can change your career:

1. You get promoted within your department
2. You move to another department (at the same level)
3. You move to another company (at the same level)

Notice that for points 2 and 3, we stated "at the same level". There are many exceptions of course, but we are referring to what's most likely. What you have within your own department is trust. The promoting manager within your existing team already knows your personality and skills first hand and is confident that you have what it takes to do the higher-level job.

The promoting managers of other departments haven't developed this level of trust in you just yet. Hiring managers of other companies have limited trust in you, simply because they don't know you at all. This can be easily overcome if you've networked with these folks, or if you have someone as a referral source in the other company who is trustworthy and highly recommends you for the job. (You see why networking is so important?) Normally, promoting managers of other departments and hiring managers of other companies only trust you enough to believe that that you can do the job you currently have. If you were an administrative assistant in the marketing department, we trust that you can do the same job in the sales department. This of course is based on probability. Recruiters may also appreciate that you have transferable skills at a new available position where the job title is completely different from your existing one.

Now by no means are we discouraging moving departments or companies. Although it may be a horizontal move, if there is more opportunity in that other place in the future, by all means take the leap. You may not be happy in your current job for whatever reason—bad manager, pay, commute, no growth, etc. But before you make the leap, research the new position or company to see if it's going to be worth the move. You don't want to jump from the frying pan into the fire, and don't be quick to assume that there's no growth where you are now, until you've read the next section.

So, let's talk about your own department, the place where a promotion is most likely. There are two kinds of employees:

The followers are those who come into the office and do what they're told to do by their managers. They come to work on time, attend all meetings on time, follow instructions to a T and meet all the goals and objectives set by their manager.

The initiators are those who come into the office and do what they're told to do by their managers. They come to work on time, attend all meetings on time, follow instructions to a T and meet all the goals and objectives set by their manager. Then they go above an beyond by taking the initiative to come up with constructive 'we' ideas and discuss them with their manager, get the buy-in and follow through with an action plan of their idea.

You already know which of the two is geared for a promotion. Now there is nothing wrong with being a follower. In fact, managers need followers on their team, the folks who diligently do the jobs that were created to solve a known problem. But if you're ever asking yourself *Why am I not getting promoted?* ask yourself the follow-up question, *What I have I done that's above and beyond my original job description?* If the answer to that question is nothing, you've proven that you are good at doing the original job that was assigned to you, but you haven't proven that you're capable of doing more. In his book *Who Gets Promoted, Who Doesn't, and Why,* career consultant Donald Asher shares stories of what he proudly calls "fast track careerists," and the difference between managing your career and experiencing it. These career fanatics make a habit of anticipating, adapting and positioning themselves with the changes in an organization, and this is how they leapfrog past others in their careers. They don't just wait for opportunities to fall into their laps. They hunt those opportunities down—and at times, even *create* them. There is a difference between *experiencing* your career and *managing* your career. Fast track careerists balance a portion of their day managing their careers by being initiators, while most others experience their careers by being followers the whole time.

Your manager may play a part in your career development. He or she may present you with opportunities to prove yourself and take the initiative to show your stuff. That's good leadership. But don't expect every manager to be this way. Generally, good leadership is hard to find. Remember, your manager is also an employee just like you, taking initiatives of his or her own to try and prove themselves to their manager and thereby to be promoted. Your boss may not have the time or the drive to present you with opportunities.

If you want that promotion, it's up to you to turn yourself from a follower into an initiator. Asking for promotions and saying that you can do it, is simply not enough. A key takeaway from *Who Gets Promoted, Who Doesn't, and Why* is that a promotion is not a reward, it's a prediction—meaning employers are not rewarding stronger performers for the past contributions. Instead, they are investing in these employees' future contributions based on abilities that they've proven to have. You have to prove that over and above your default job description, you've initiated and implemented constructive 'we' ideas that align with the department's objectives and future changes. Don't wait for your manager to spoon-feed these to you. And remember, an idea is just a thought until it comes to life with an action plan. We've seen it one too many times, employees coming up with great ideas, and leaving it at that. Don't bother voicing an idea if you have no intent of bringing it to life. That's where you run the risk of being perceived as lazy by your manager. You may also think that your default job takes up one hundred per cent of your time and you simply don't have the capacity to take initiatives. Well, while that excuse keeps you anchored as a follower, somebody else having the same job as you, is working weekends from home or an extra hour after or before their shift, taking initiatives and setting the wheels in motion to sail away with that eventual promotion.

So now that you've understood the need to position yourself as an initiator in the eyes of management, what comes next? *You anticipate change and grab an opportunity to rise.* No matter how many problems management solves by creating positions like the one you're in, new problems always rear their ugly heads. What follows is key. The managers then try to solve these problems with the existing staff—and this is where you come in. With your constructive 'we' ideas and action plans that solve these problems, they see you as an employee capable of fulfilling more than your current job description. Eventually, they may realize that these new problems will never go away, so now they need to create a *new* position to address these problems. And who do you think is going to be on the top of their list to fill this role? This is one way that you can be promoted within the department.

Then of course, there's the time when someone on the team has to leave the department, and his or her role needs to be filled. Management *always* prefers hiring from within, because it's less risky and cheaper (as minimal training will be needed). Outside of political influence (let's not rule that out, this is a cut-throat corporate world after all), the gap will be filled by the person who has already demonstrated his or her capabilities that align with the requirements of this vacant position. But if no one on the inside has demonstrated this thus far, the hiring manager will (sadly) place their trust in an external candidate over the disappointed members of the team.

Here's a story of how Cornelius, an emerging Millennial, managed his career. His entry level job as an IT engineer involved fixing the typical IT issues faced by employees in the office. As he was the only one doing this work, his job was nearly full time. Once Cornelius got into the groove of the day-to-day work, he realized that procurement was a challenge for the company. Finance required the creation of reports with specific amounts calculated from the budget before a purchase could be made. This was a cumbersome task. With a little coding know-how and a lot of Googling, this engineer created a little program in Microsoft Access that streamlined the procurement process. His manager was very impressed.

Demonstrating this application also caught wider attention. The finance team then approached him and stated that a lot of payments needed to be forecasted for budget management purposes. Cornelius then incorporated financial reports into his application and started to develop relationships with these vendors, even finding new ones that offered more flexible credit agreements. Now the finance team was impressed too. Eventually, the company grew in size and with more employees, the IT team needed to expand. Since the IT department reported to the finance department, management decided to hire another IT engineer to handle most of the grunt work of supporting end users. Cornelius was promoted to Assistant IT Manager, supporting the new engineer when needed, but focusing more on finance and procurement. He was also given the opportunity to manage budgets.

As time went on and the company grew, they hired an IT director to oversee all of IT operations. This boss of Cornelius's boss restructured the department, placing emphasis on supporting the region as a whole. Cornelius was introduced to other IT engineers in the region and proactively engaged in discussions with them. Because his procurement process application was such a huge success, they incorporated it into the region as well. Cornelius reached out to the other IT engineers in the region to learn what pain points they were experiencing in their environment. He developed a constructive idea to tackle all those issues, and set up meetings with the manager and the director to discuss them.

Eventually, the director authorized Cornelius to travel to these countries in the region to train those engineers and improve their IT processes.

As the company and the region grew, Cornelius developed more constructive 'we' ideas that supported the entire team. But his boss, the IT manager, was falling behind. With his usual laidback attitude, he couldn't keep up with the rapid expansion. Eventually, the IT director had to let go of the IT manager due to lack of performance. Guess who got the job? They hired another IT engineer in the team, which completely alleviated all of the grunt work of IT, and Cornelius focused primarily on vendor management, financial management, and mentoring his IT engineers as required—the typical responsibilities of most managers.

Create your own opportunities

Sarah Blakely, CEO of Spanks, once said, "The more you experience in life, the more you have to offer others." That resonates with us. We encourage you to take advantage of opportunities when they come your way, and if they don't come your way, reach out and make them happen. Volunteering and joining professional communities are ideal ways to make this happen.

We've grown up in an age where the Internet has kept the world at our fingertips. While this has allowed us to be more connected to the world, it has also created an easier path for us to connect with others. (It's definitely easier to text someone because it's quick and instant.) But one thing has not changed in our world—the value of personal human connection. Opportunities will always be handled by the person you met or spoke with, rather than the person you texted. Hey, if there were no value in human connection anymore, there wouldn't be a need for a personal job interview, right?

Even within your own company, opportunities exist to make parallel moves to other departments. The only way you can seize these opportunities is to be noticed and network with the people in these departments, so they'll remember you when an opportunity comes up. Pay attention to what's happening around you in the business. Don't just be tethered to your own department. Promotions to other departments can only happen if the other department *knows you exist*.

While the job track process you followed in chapter 6 was focused on publicly advertised jobs, the same principles apply in your applications to internal vacancies in the company. Although the hiring process may not be as broken internally, depending on the size of your organization, the principles of *competition*, *standing out*, *reaching out directly* and *getting personal* with people are as relevant as ever.

The Aon Hewitt 2016 Workforce Mindset Study shows that when compared to Gen X, Millennials rank career opportunities as a higher priority than benefits. These opportunities are not going to fall into your lap. Actively network and conquer your fears of reaching out and starting conversations with strangers. This way, you will make those opportunities happen for yourself.

The Toastmasters club that John belongs to inspired him to deliver 300 speeches in 2016. It's a challenge that he took on to meet certain personal goals and commitments. Others were motivated by his accomplishment, which presented him with even more opportunities within the organization. This professional community encourages him to get out of his comfort zone and do things that he wouldn't normally do. This has been noticed by his community peers. John's challenge has been spoken about and referenced in other speeches, really making him proud of what he's accomplishing. During the times when his workplace does not help him to feel motivated or accomplished, this professional community reminds him that he is fulfilling his purpose. Everyone needs to belong an organization that does this.

Don't ever underestimate the value of human connection, as terrifying as that might seem. In your workplace, compliment directors on their department's achievements, ask other managers questions about their experience, ask team leads for an opportunity to shadow them to understand their jobs. You lose nothing by asking! If you don't ask, you're losing out to the competition—someone else who *does* have the courage to reach out to people directly. That person is the one being hired for the job, the one being promoted, and the one being assigned the new projects. If you put yourself out there, at some point, life will hand you something back and that's when things will really start to change.

CHAPTER 12

THE MILLENNIAL DIFFERENCE

It's time to congratulate yourself on coming this far into the book. We hope that you've learned a new approach to grabbing the next job that's right for you, because you deserve to be in that position. As Millennials, we have so much to offer this world and *we* are going to be the ones to really change it. Being held back by student debt and bank loans prevents us from reaching our potential. Dedicating ourselves to a meaningful purpose 40 hours a week—be it as an employee or even someday as an entrepreneur—is what we hope you will accomplish after completing this book.

We would like to conclude with this chapter on awareness—about who we are as Millennials, about how we are viewed in the workplace, and about the strengths and weaknesses that we can work to our advantage, or work around, to move forward.

The Gallup Report that we have used as a source for this book received a thought-provoking comment from Gallup's CEO Jim Clifton: "Are Millennials really that different? The answer is yes—profoundly so. Millennials will change the world decisively more than any other generation."

Job hopping

We don't discourage moving between jobs. In fact, one of the themes of this book is to create job security that allows you to be considered hirable by many companies at any time. Millennial career expert and author Adam "Smiley" Poswolsky, in his book *Quarter Life Breakthrough*, endorses moving jobs if that's what it takes to discover your true calling and passion in life. A fantastic read, the book is written specifically for Millennials trying to discover themselves.

However, it's important to understand how job hoppers are viewed in the eyes of the hiring manager. While working in different fields is commendable, as it exposes you to a wider scope in terms of experience, the practice of changing jobs every year may not be. In this case, the hiring manager may only see you as a short-term hire, and that's never a good thing.

The exception, of course, is self-employed contractors, where your primary reason for moving jobs is simply that your contract expired. But with full-time jobs, make sure that you have a *good reason* for the job change. Research shows that most Millennials change jobs because they don't feel that their work is fulfilling or allowing them to maximize their potential. If you've tried your best, especially following the suggestions in the previous chapter, and you still feel that what you do is unfulfilling, it's time to move on. But make sure you secure a worthy reason at the interview. "I was bored" won't impress the hiring manager. Something along the lines of: "I feel that I gained everything I could out of this job, and I don't see any potential for me in my current role anymore—so I'm seeking a change and a new challenge" sounds more appealing and meaningful.

If you're planning on changing jobs, be sure to seriously reflect on your motivations for doing so. It's well known that most people don't leave companies—they leave managers. You may not like your manager's character—remember that it's rare to find real leaders in organizations—but ask yourself whether your manager is really the reason for you not experiencing a meaningful career in your current company. Does this person deny you carrying out your ideas *all* the time? Has he or she given you any opportunity to do something different? If not, why didn't it happen? Was it *your manager* or was it *you*? Did you voice your concerns to your manager when it was appropriate or did you just bottle it up? It's easy to blame your boss when you aren't feeling fulfilled, because it's easy to bottle things up and find excuses to not carry out an idea. But, it's also possible that your boss truly is a micro-managing, spotlight-stealing, finger-pointing, idea-trashing ass. In which case, it's a good reason to find work elsewhere.

According to the Deloitte Millennial survey, it's not just managers that are accountable for staff turnover; the organization itself has a role to play in gaining our trust and loyalty. The survey reveals that 76 per cent of Millennials now regard businesses as an influential force for positive social impact. They believe that companies should, for the most part, be responsible for creating social optimism. 86 per cent believe that the success of a business should be measured in terms of more than just its financial performance, with added focus on education, skills and training, unemployment issues, healthcare, disease prevention, and other such social concerns and attributes. Apart from social responsibility, organizations should also strive to keep their people informed about what's going on, and encourage their executive leadership team to cascade information down through their respective teams and foster a culture of involvement. Organizations that take an *inclusive approach* are less likely to lose people.

Finding purpose

One of the biggest differences with the millennial generation is that purpose is valued over money. Indeed, research has shown that

Millennials are willing to take a pay cut if it means finding a job that is more meaningful to them and aligns with their purpose. We are willing to make sacrifices to get things that money cannot buy. This is probably the most challenging Millennial trait for management to meet, and HR management is aware of its importance. You may see it on employee surveys: "Do you feel that you are making a difference to the organization?"

It's difficult to believe that you can influence change in an organization, especially when you are one person among thousands, a cog in a complex machine. And from the company's perspective, you *are* expendable. Let's not deny it. You were hired to solve a problem. That is the purpose of your job. The question is, does that purpose align with yours? Adam Poswolsky's book *The Quarter-Life Breakthrough* is truly about finding purpose in your life and how you may not know what your purpose is at this very moment. With every job you have, you will discover something new about yourself—and it may not even be related to the actual work you do.

> From Connel's last job change, he moved from a technical position where two people reported to him to an administration position where fifteen people reported to him. His new responsibilities were to lead people, to encourage his staff to reach their potential, and to keep them motivated and engaged in their work. As he shared his knowledge and suggestions with them and saw them put it into action and achieve results. Connel also found himself motivated to experiment with coaching and mentoring techniques. He had discovered a new purpose, which was to help others define their goals and reach their potential. This had nothing to do with the department or the company's purpose, but it was a personal purpose that he discovered with his new role.

Perhaps you may not be so fortunate to find your ultimate purpose at your current job, or maybe even at the next three jobs that you have. But what's important to note for this section is that while many companies try to align their purpose with its employees, there are too many variables and hurdles in the way for you to *sit around* and expect it to happen. Seek out your purpose yourself. Don't wait for the company or the department or even your manager to give it to you. If your boss is a true leader and a mentor, you may get help to find it. But never count on it. At a public speaking event on *passion* that we recently attended, one of the speakers talked about purpose. We'll never forget a statement he made: "The two most important days of your life are the day you were born and the day you realized why."

Work to your strengths

Here's a little déjà vu from the interview chapters: what *are* your strengths? You should have a few in mind, but chances are that just like your purpose, you may not have discovered your strengths yet. But given time, you will. They will come to you one strength at a time.

In the mean time, work with what you know. If you're aware of your strengths, you are probably aware of your weaknesses too. Companies are trying to adopt a strength-based approach with their employees, and so should you. Related to your job, you may be juggling the following traits:

1. Strengths that relate to your job: Focus on these and keep working at these. They come most easily to you and also create the biggest impact.
2. Strengths that don't relate to your job: If you are aware of a strength that you unfortunately don't find many opportunities to demonstrate, you should use them when required. Your manager may also perceive this as a strength in you and encourage you to use it. But don't count on it.
3. Weaknesses that relate to your job: If you find yourself battling a weakness that you encounter every day, the best advice is to avoid this kind of work altogether if possible. This is the

objective of the strength-based approach that companies are trying to adopt. Consider delegating that task to someone else or approaching your manager and requesting an alternate option. That being said, we don't encourage ignoring all of your weaknesses either. There are some weaknesses that you must work on for the betterment of yourself and your career. Avoiding confrontation is a common weakness that folks have. Developing your emotional intelligence can help you to manage this.

4. Weaknesses that don't relate to your job: Why bother with these at work?

Mentors and coaches

Let's cover the definitions first. Although mentoring and coaching have been used interchangeably, and some people have successfully worn both hats, there are differences between the two. A coach is someone who will guide you on the right path to accomplishing a task or several tasks or a goal in general. There is usually a short-term objective that ends once the task or goal is accomplished. Coaches are not subject matter experts in your field. They work with your own potential and skills to help you reach a solution.

Working with a mentor however, is a long-term relationship. A mentor is someone you wish to emulate, not just for one specific task or goal, but even in terms of technical expertise, approach and methodology, and strengths of character, judgement, etc. Mentors are subject matter experts in your field, and they most likely walked in your shoes at some point in their career.

Mentors and coaches share the knowledge and expertise they've accumulated through years of experience. At the workplace, a coach might be a colleague or a senior team member who can guide you in achieving your potential in your role. A mentor could be a manager or director who was in your position several years ago whose great success at it has led to a position of authority. How did my mentor do it? What do I need to do to get there? These are some of the questions you may ask yourself in that relationship.

The research shows that Millennials want their managers to play more of a mentorship and coaching role over a traditional manager's role. In practical terms, Millennials don't want a command-and-direct, my-way-or-the-highway attitude from their managers. They expect a certain degree of autonomy and the freedom to make their own choices, guided by the experience and wisdom of their managers.

Indeed, this expectation is certainly being promoted as an ideal in the workplace. Countless articles and blogs on leadership that are directed at managers endorse the same approach to managing staff. It's great to know what's needed from you as a leader, but to achieve it is a different story altogether. Leadership is brought into this section because being a coach or a mentor significantly develops the characteristics of a leader. The ability to be an authentic leader is tied closely to your personality. We believe that a selfless desire to serve and to make sacrifices for another human being is required to be a leader. Do you think this comes easily to most people? Do you think that most managers would be willing to put aside their own work and agenda to prioritize the needs of each individual member of their team? After attaining a wealth of experience and knowledge through self-sacrifice and hard work, would they be willing to share it freely with others?

We've had some great mentors—managers and directors whose personality and work ethic we found ourselves mirroring, with whom we've had many discussions and from whom we have learned something new. For the most part, we can rely on free knowledge from the Internet as well as formal training that we bankroll to enhance our knowledge and expertise. We can train ourselves to overcome knowledge hurdles, but also learn from mentors to overcome the real-world hurdles. If you find yourself lacking coaches or mentors in your current job, don't stew in your own misfortune or think that's a reason to quit your job and find something else. We live in a digital world with limitless resources of knowledge at our fingertips, and if it's a mentor you're looking for, we encourage you to use resources such as **http://www.mentorcity.com**.

At the very least, if you've not yet discovered a formal coach or a mentor in your life, you have probably met *somebody* in your life who was successful and who's personality resonated with you. It doesn't necessarily have to be someone in your line of work. It could even be a parent or sibling. If you get an opportunity, talk to this person and ask how he or she achieved success.

Work-life balance

Our Gen X and Baby Boomer colleagues, for the most part, spent the earlier years of their career frequently burning the midnight oil, working late hours where quantity of hours were considered hard work. Millennials, with our deep thirst for knowledge, believe in working smart; that is, working shorter hours and achieving the same results or more. This allows us the time to enjoy our personal lives with family and friends as well as the pursuit of personal interests and hobbies.

Although we (John and Connel) did spend the very early paying-our-dues years working late nights alongside Gen Xers and Boomers, we believe that it's imperative to set your clock to the eight hours for which you are paid to work. As your work day goes by, you start to burn out and you're not very productive beyond a certain point. Use time management techniques and stick to your schedule so you can also pursue a fulfilling life outside of work. If things aren't going right outside the office, you will bring that anxiety to work as well, and your performance will suffer.

Performance reviews

As we write this book, one of the strategies in corporate management news is how certain companies are thinking ahead and getting rid of the performance review process. An HR methodology that's been around for years, the performance review subjectively or quantitatively *measures* your on-the-job performance to justify your bonus or salary increase—or whether you will keep your job!

Yes, for many jobs, there are numerical measurements that can be used to assess performance. Sales employees are measured against the dollar value of revenue they produce; credit control employees are measured against the receivable amounts that were collected; call centre employees are often measured by the number of calls they've handled on average every month. *But how can you measure things like innovation, personal development, reliability and initiative?* These are certainly qualities that your manager desires of you, yet they do not contribute to the measure of your performance.

Naturally, good managers see past the performance review metrics and also take into account the other qualities you possess. However, we stand alongside the research and the new initiatives being taken by forward-thinking companies, recognizing that Millennials don't want to have performance reviews anymore. They would rather have ongoing conversations with their managers to discuss their performance, including what they're doing right and how they can improve. We've experienced this firsthand with the Millennials we manage. They are eager to ask, "So how am I doing? What do you think I can do to improve?" We love having these conversations—they provide a chance for us to put on our coaching cap. And we respect our staff by being honest, open and up front. According to the Aon Workforce Mindset Study, as far as performance management goes, Gen X prefers their managers to have more hands-on involvement, whereas Millennials are more independent. They just want their managers to care about them and their work rather than focus on numbers.

Now, don't expect the next company you join to be on the bandwagon with those forward-thinking companies that are doing away with performance reviews. Companies such as General Electric, Adobe and Netflix have already taken the performance review process out of their culture. Chances are, the company you are or will be working in is very much still committed to its traditional HR best practices of performance reviews. Furthermore, you may also not have the kind of manager who will proactively schedule sit-down conversations with you to discuss your performance on a regular basis. Therefore, make the effort to initiate these conversations yourself. If you approach your boss and ask, "Can we have a chat when you're free?" you engage your manager and steer him or her to look beyond the boundaries of the traditional performance review when the time comes. But please remember to be considerate of your manager's schedule and time. After all, that person's job also comes with its own list of responsibilities. A performance conversation once a month should be more than enough. Anything more, and these frequent requests might give off an "Are we there yet?" vibe.

Learning and development

It is said that mastery in your field of expertise is a strong motivator for anyone, and we Millennials, with our thirst for knowledge, yearn to learn and develop ourselves. In whatever field you find yourself, there is no end to what you can learn about it. Constant research fuels new information, and people who are passionate about the subject globally write blogs about their field, citing their own opinions and recommendations.

Many people believe that experience has taught them to be subject matter experts. Undeniably, experience carries a lot of weight, and many people have succeeded in learning through experience alone. But why not combine research-based learning and experience? Unless you're in the field of research yourself and at the pinnacle of your career, we believe that whatever you do, someone else has done it better. Why reinvent the wheel? Learn what they have done, and then customize it to your own unique situation. That's combining knowledge and experience.

If it's knowledge that you seek, don't wait for your management to present it to you on a silver platter. If you work in a large corporation, take advantage of any learning and development program that is available to you. And development, doesn't just mean learning the technical aspects of your job. John and Connel, for example, took formal training courses in IT service management, but have also learned about project management, public speaking, time management, coaching and leadership through a variety of methods that include formal classroom training courses, online webinars, reading a Kindle on the bus and listening to an audio book in the car.

But here's the kicker: *Education and knowledge mean nothing if you don't apply them to your life or your job.* In reality, you may not be able to apply everything you read, but if you can apply just *one* thing from each learning material, it's worth the effort.

From reading Kevin Kruse's '15 secrets successful people know about time man-agement', one very important lesson that we learned was that working with emails is the least productive activity you can do in the office. This hit home hard because that's where we felt we were spending most of our time. So now, we have turned off email notifications and we schedule one or two hours per day on email, care-fully placed at the end of our day or during lunch. And it has worked! We are much more productive and feel that we accomplish more with our time.

Grab the bull by the horns and seek out knowledge yourself. A published author is someone who has written about subjects that have been tried and tested. Master the basics of your job by learning from others, and experiment with the finer points to create your own unique experiences.

Being patient

The strangest conversation we've ever had with an employee followed from him saying, "I expect to be promoted every six months." When we asked him about his action plan to achieve such an ambitious goal, he had none. In the book *Who Gets Promoted, Who Doesn't and Why*, Donald Asher writes about his interviews with people who have career changes and promotions every 12 to 24 months. These people all have a vision and a plan to where they want to go next in their careers.

Your career will take time to reach its potential, even with consistent effort. If you've followed everything we've suggested in these last few chapters, your career, just like a tree, will still need time and constant nourishment to grow. There are things in life—relationships, investments, mastery of skills and yes, your career—that are not at all like Amazon Prime or Netflix or Apple Music. There is no 'on demand' or 'one-click buy' to success. Think of the years of struggle and effort you went through to get your diploma or degree in school. You accepted that there were no short cuts and no cutting corners. Your objective was to stick to it and get it done. The same goes for your career, except it's going to take a lot more effort and a lot more time. At least you're being paid while you achieve it!

Becoming a "fast-track careerist", as Donald Asher calls it, requires a certain know-how that you can develop with time *if* you actively seek it. Patiently and *consistently* learn skills in networking, technical knowledge, relationship development and understanding how others think, and you will start to gain momentum toward that career you desire.

Being engaged

Finally, we sum up all of the above points under one very important message to you, both for yourself and your manager's perspective: *Be engaged with your job*. Managers know instantly who among their team members are engaged and who aren't. This demarcation is so important, that the research on Millennials in the workforce actually distinguishes the engaged staff from the disengaged staff, presumably because the numbers vary so drastically between the two. The Gallup Report on How Millennials want to Work and Live states that only 29 per cent of Millennials are engaged in their jobs, while 16 per cent are actively disengaged, meaning that they are unhappy, acting out, and capable of damaging the morale of their coworkers as well as harming their company in some way.

The following table lists behaviours of an engaged or disengaged employee:

Topic	Engaged ☺	Disengaged ☹
Feedback	Voluntarily provides constructive feedback about the job he/she is doing, and any positive or negative aspects that should be encouraged or fixed.	Never provides feedback freely, and may only speak up when asked in a one-on-one meeting. These are not signs of being an introvert—even introverts give feedback if they are engaged.

Topic	Engaged ☺	Disengaged ☹
Ideas	Always comes up with new ideas and shares them with the manager or the team. All ideas don't have to be great or implemented, but this person is never discouraged from voicing new ideas.	Almost never comes up with new ideas. Follows along with whatever the team comes up with. May give an opinion on a new idea if asked.
Absenteeism	Rarely claims the one-day sick leave during the year.	Often claims the one-day sick leave, especially on a Monday or Friday.
Solutionist	Comes to the table with a problem, a solution, and a proposed action plan.	Comes to the table with a problem, a complaint, and a reason for being unable to do the job.
Ownership	"I will take care of it."	"It's not my job."
Initiative	Doesn't wait for the manager to come up with tasks to be given. Creates his/her own work from productive ideas with the manager's buy-in. Tries to learn new things with formal or informal training.	Is happy spending two hours a day on Facebook, rather than creating new work. Is content with current knowledge that he/she has acquired through experience.
Scope	Is not afraid to take on challenges that are outside of the original job.	As long as it's not in the original job description, the employee either avoids or outright refuses to do it.

Topic	Engaged ☺	Disengaged ☹
Sacrifice	Is willing to take one for the team. If it means doing an extra shift or working over time, has an "it's a tough job but someone's got to do it" attitude.	Clocks in and out at exactly eight hours, regardless of the condition of the team. Does not go the extra mile.
Quality	Has mastered the basics of the job and is ready to take on more challenges.	Is still struggling with the basics of the job, and takes no initiative or interest to improve, unless given an ultimatum.

The above examples are by no means exhaustive, but are certainly the leading signs, in our experience, that demonstrate an employee's engagement and passion for his or her job. Make no mistake, managers can easily spot the difference. Whether you are looking for work or are currently at a job, take the time to reflect on the above behaviours and ask yourself where you stand on each of these. If you are currently on a team, you may have noticed that your manager pays more attention to one or two of the team members more than others. Why? Perhaps those team members are flourishing in many of the above examples.

Take an honest look at your position in the job, and if you find yourself possessing the qualities of a disengaged employee, it's time to turn things around. There maybe a good reason for your disengagement as well—perhaps you don't get a long with the people around you, or your job is just not fulfilling your purpose—in which case, it's time for a job or career change. If you want to be engaged and move ahead, keep in mind that what's in your job description is a comfort zone that you need to break out of. Managers notice employees who go the extra mile and prove that they are capable of doing more than what their told to do.

Leading tomorrow's Centennials

When we started this book, we had one goal in mind: to help emerging Millennials embark on their careers as quickly as possible with a stronger foundation than they currently have and with information that no college or university would have taught them. We also wanted to help established Millennials, already with some years of experience, understand how to create their own job security and reach their potential in the work place.

As we write this book, we accept that we are far from achieving our own purposes. We have held mid-level management positions and responsibilities and have made a habit out of being engaged and encouraging other people to succeed. This book is our way of sharing our knowledge in hopes that Millennials and others seeking meaningful work are inspired to succeed—by using our collective experience and advice as a guide and creating their own paths to success. With time, Millennials will dominate the workforce, but for now we are going through a transition phase where Generation X meets Generation Y (Millennials). We've worked almost exclusively with Gen X management and ourselves currently lead Millennials. With all the negative vibes between generations, we felt it was time to bridge the gap and create an understanding.

You now know what to expect from Gen X, and remember that it's not a question of better or worse, right or wrong. Thanks to the Internet, the world is transforming at an exponential rate and it's understandable that there are be large disparities between working styles of the two generations. We will continue to be in this transition phase for the next decade at least, and it's important to know how to play the Gen X-Y game if you want to succeed. Since the majority of the decision-making positions today are held by Gen Xers and Boomers, we hope this book will guide you to that next stepping stone in your career. On this path, you will become tomorrow's leaders, and in turn, pave the way for people like our daughters, Generation Z—the Centennials!

Disregard the negative labels the world puts on you. According to the Deloitte Millennial Survey conducted around the world, these are the main areas of advice Millennials would give to Gen Z:

1. Learn as much as possible.
2. Work hard.
3. Be patient.
4. Be dedicated.
5. Be flexible.

We couldn't be more pleased with this generation. Advice given by Millennials to Centennials varies by country, but the most common advice from the U.S. and Canada was to work hard. No matter which generation you are part of, the one thing that never changes is that hard work always pays off. It doesn't start from the day you enter an office. You hustled from the day you started school and you interned and volunteered during that period. You hustled yourself through the job search period by standing out and reaching out. And you continue hustling in your work and your career by focusing on your goals every day. You are constantly developing and learning. Never be afraid to try new things, experiment and reach out to people directly on the way.

Yes, you will make mistakes. But it's just as important to make those mistakes because then you learn what you *don't* want to do in life, and that's never a waste of time. At least you were in control of your own mistake, and if you have made every effort to develop yourself along your career, you can live and learn from the mistakes you make. Our favourite quote on this subject is: "Put yourself out of business, because if you don't someone else will!" (Gary Vaynerchuk) Remember when John's department was being outsourced? We were being put out of business then. In six months, 25 members of our team were mentored through the interview process you have now learned, and every one of them had a new job before that six-month period was up. That's when we both realized the potential of our workforce and the importance of creating our own job security rather than relying on the loyalty of the company.

The only thing that has changed in our generation is technology and with it, the age of social networking. Use this technology to your advantage, but don't let it diminish the basic components of success— *working hard*, *direct human contact*, *trying new things* and *taking risks*. We all have our own paths and timelines for working toward our purpose. Here's an example:

> Experiment and try new things and discover yourself in your 20s. Learn from your mistakes, find your purpose, and develop your skills in your 30s. Build upon on your purpose and master your skills in your 40s. Ride the wave of success in your 50s, helping others along the way. "Retire" in your 60s. This's doesn't mean stop working. Rather, it means that fulfilling your purposes is no longer a monetary obligation. *It's a choice!*

Success comes to those who go through these milestones, and the superstars achieve them more quickly than others do. We hope this book gets you there as soon as possible so that our community, society and economy benefits from the purpose you discover in your career and life.

John Ribeiro & Connel Valentine

APPENDIX A

Survey references

Aon Hewitt 2016 Workforce Mindset Study
http://www.aon.com/human-capital-consulting/thought-leadership/communication/2016-workforce-mindset.jsp

Deloitte Millennial Survey 2017
https://www2.deloitte.com/global/en/pages/about-deloitte/articles/millennialsurvey.html

Gallup report on How Millennials Want to Work and Live
http://www.gallup.com/reports/189830/millennials-work-live.aspx

Jobvite 2016 Recruiter Nation Survey
http://www.jobvite.com/resources/ebooks/2016_recruiter_nation_survey/

National Society of High School Scholars 2016 Millennial Career Survey
https://nshss.org/newsroom/millennial-career-survey/

Statistics Canada Labour Force Survey (January 2017 release)
http://www.statcan.gc.ca/daily-quotidien/170210/dq170210a-eng.htm

Statistics Canada Tuition Fees for Degree Programs (2016/2017 release)
http://www.statcan.gc.ca/daily-quotidien/160907/dq160907a-eng.htm

Statistics Canada University Tuition Fees (2015/2016 release)
http://www.statcan.gc.ca/daily-quotidien/150909/dq150909b-eng.htm

Toronto Employment Survey 2016
http://www1.toronto.ca/wps/portal/contentonly?vgnextoid=c7ac186e20ee0410VgnVCM10000071d60f89RCRD

APPENDIX B

Reading references

15 Secrets that Successful People Know about Time Management by Kevin Kruse
https://www.kevinkruse.com/

8000hours.org blog on job satisfaction
https://80000hours.org/career-guide/job-satisfaction/

Career Planning and Adult Development Journal
https://www.job-hunt.org/CPAD-Journal-32Number2-PersonalSEO.pdf

Emotional Intelligence 2.0 by Travis Bradberry and Jean Greaves

How to Use Facebook for Professional Networking
http://theundercoverrecruiter.com/how-use-facebook-professional-networking-10-useful-tips/

Knock 'em Dead by Martin Yate
https://knockemdead.com

The Muse – 31 Attention-Grabbing Cover Letter Examples
https://www.themuse.com/advice/31-attentiongrabbing-cover-letter-examples

The Quarter-life Breakthrough by Adam Smiley Poswolsky
http://www.thequarterlifebreakthrough.com/

Who Gets Promoted, Who Doesn't and Why by Donald Asher
http://www.donaldasher.com/

APPENDIX C

Website references

Amy Cuddy Ted Talk on body language
https://www.youtube.com/watch?v=Ks-_Mh1QhMc&t=5s

Building your online resume
http://www.wix.com
http://www.wordpress.com

Check your typing speed
http://www.typingtest.com

Finding common interest groups
http://www.meetup.com

Finding an online mentor
http://www.mentorcity.com

Infographics on the career progression of leaders
http://fundersandfounders.com/

Key small business statistics
http://www.ic.gc.ca/eic/site/061.nsf/eng/h_03018.html

Reviews on organizational culture
https://www.glassdoor.ca/index.htm

Searching for target jobs
http://www.onetonline.org

ACKNOWLEDGEMENTS

John Ribeiro

I have finally reached a point in my life where I am ready to share stories and experiences that I have learned over the years. Looking back, I realize that I did not do it alone. This book would not have come together if it weren't for my family and friends who have supported me through the process.

To my wife Dianne, my biggest supporter, I am grateful that you are here to share this adventure with me. To the kids, Julian, Amanda and Alexia, thank you for putting up with my talks and listening to all the stories about finding work. I know it will come in handy for you one day. Many thanks to my friends Sandro, Lucia and Matthew who have provided moral support and encouragement throughout the writing of this book.

The biggest thank you goes to my co-author and good friend Connel Valentine. You are one of the hardest-working Millennials that I know. You have put all the pieces together and have made this book a reality. I am grateful that our paths have crossed and look forward to sharing in our future successes together.

Connel Valentine

Three dates I can never forget are the day my daughter was born, the day I got married, and the day I migrated to Canada. Among many things, this book is a reward for crossing these milestones in my life, and I give my sincerest thanks to my wife Renita and daughter Katelyn for inspiring me during this mission. My thanks also go to my dad and mom Edgar and Prescilla, my brother and sister Selwyn and Fallon, and all my in-laws who are cheering me on from way out in Dubai. Leaving them to migrate to Canada was the hardest thing I've ever had to do in my life, and this book is a reminder of their support and love.

Last but not least, my thanks and gratitude to my co-author and mentor John Ribeiro who planted the seed for this book and will bring it to the hearts and minds of the Millennials who need it the most. Without his encouragement and guidance, I would not be striving to reach my potential as I am today.

Special Thanks

To Sandro Parisotto, who shared his creativity with his design of our amazing book cover.

To Lucia Bellefante, who beta read our manuscript, and supported and encouraged our efforts with her experience and insight.

To John Guan, a fellow Millennial who does his generation proud with his creative eye and technical wizardry in developing our stunning website, **www.zero2hired.com**.

ABOUT THE AUTHORS

John Ribeiro was born and raised in Toronto, Ontario, Canada. As a first-generation Canadian, he knows first hand the struggles of getting into the workforce. He completed his Marketing Diploma program at Seneca College in 1995. Unfortunately, finding work after graduation was a challenge, so he returned to Seneca and enrolled in the new Internet and Electronic Commerce program. After graduation, he started his corporate career with one of Canada's largest telecom companies as an entry-level Technical Support Technician. His goal was to make it through Y2K and then find "something better". Working for this organization "only on a temporary basis" turned out to be 18 years and counting. During his tenure, John has had the opportunity to manage all types of teams, from developers to first-line support staff. His goal in hiring team members is always to make sure he has the right person for the role. This book is a sum of all the insight he has gained over the years in hiring. John shares with you the nuts and bolts of acing the interview. The guidance provided in this book is guaranteed to reduce the time you spend looking for work—you just have to put in the effort.

Connel Valentine was born and raised in Dubai. He graduated with a Bachelor's Degree in Computer Science and has worked in the field of IT Service Management ever since. After 33 years of living in Dubai, he decided to migrate to Canada, seeking a new home, new opportunities and a stable future for himself and his family. After a two-week vacation in Canada, absorbing the vibrant culture, the friendly people and the gorgeous summer weather of his new home, his first opportunity presented itself. Two weeks after his job hunt began, he got offered to work for one of the most reputable telecommunication companies in Canada, where he met his manager and soon-to-be co-author John Ribeiro. Today, Connel leads a team of 15 Millennials, coaching them to reach their potential. His favourite subjects of research are leadership, coaching, career development, Millennial mindset and blogging. Through this book, he hopes to inspire others to follow their heart, to live by their own standards and not by those of others, and to ultimately reach their potential.

www.ingramcontent.com/pod-product-compliance
Lightning Source LLC
Chambersburg PA
CBHW070923210326
41520CB00021B/6785